Praise for

THE MYSTERY OF CATASTROPHE

The Mystery of Catastrophe inspires and encourages the reader to embrace God's priorities and His sovereign will for the world today. The authors give helpful insight informed by their understanding and experience of God working in and through global disasters. A must read for understanding the times and making sense of what appears to be senseless. As an Albanian pastor and Evangelical I have witnessed first-hand many of the stories told in this book.

—ZEFJAN NIKOLLA, PASTOR OF EMANUEL EVANGELICAL CHURCH AND EXECUTIVE DIRECTOR OF WILBERFORCE FOUNDATION, ALBANIA

The philosophical centuries old topic of the suffering of the innocent has been one of central themes in many discourses. *The Mystery of Catastrophe* brings into light God's purpose in calamities. After the tragedy Kosovo experienced in 1999, God opened new horizons for this nation. This is a perfect example of how God will use the suffering yet to come under a new religious political ruling system of the antichrist. *The Mystery of Catastrophe* walks the reader down the eschatological road of biblical prophecies to offer meaning and hope to the suffering. This a must-read book that comes at the right time.

—PASTOR DRITON KRASNIQI, FORMER PRESIDENT OF THE KOSOVO PROTESTANT EVANGELICAL ALLIANCE

Christians have been trying to go to the ends of the earth to make disciples for years. And now God is bringing the world to Christians. *The Mystery of Catastrophe* is a profound look at how God uses catastrophes and crisis to scatter unbelievers throughout the world. This book will challenge your thinking on refugees and the end times.

— HUGH O. MACLELLAN, CHAIRMAN EMERITUS,

THE MACLELLAN FOUNDATION

The Mystery of Catastrophe is a critically important and genuinely prophetic word for this hour. Not only does it identify the great challenges of the last days, but much more importantly, it lays out a clear Gospel-centered response."

—JOSEPH FARAH, CEO WND

THE MYSTERY

of

CATASTROPHE

THE MYSTERY

of

CATASTROPHE

Understanding GOD'S REDEMPTIVE PURPOSES
for the GLOBAL DISASTERS *of the* LAST DAYS

JOEL RICHARDSON
& NATHAN GRAVES

WINEPRESS

THE MYSTERY OF CATASTROPHE

Book designed by Mark Karis

Hardcover ISBN: 978-1-949729-00-9
eBook ISBN: 978-1-949729-03-0

Printed in the United States of America

To my wife, Lorraine, the love of my life, and to the greatest earthly gifts God ever gave to me—my two sons, Josiah and Justin

Contents

Acknowledgements

I WANT TO THANK my Savior Jesus Christ first of all, for so great a salvation He lavished on me and for putting this book in my heart. I thank my wife, Lorraine, for all her prayers, encouragement, support, and helpful insights. Special thanks to James Beery, my dear and precious friend, mentor, high school football coach, and English teacher who gave me a love for writing and has modeled for me the life of a godly man. Finally, I want to thank Joel Richardson, a man of God who believed in me, supported me, and gave me this amazing opportunity to share with you what burns deeply in my heart.

NATHAN GRAVES

AS ALWAYS, I would like to thank my wife, Amy, for her unwavering support. Many thanks to Geoffrey Stone for your critical assistance and editorial oversight. It's deeply appreciated. Much thanks to Mark Karis for another great cover design. To all those partners who continue to support the work the Lord has given us to accomplish, and who so faithfully cover my family and me in prayer, I simply cannot thank you enough. May the Lord return all of the blessings that you've given to me back on to you in multiplied abundance. Finally, thanks to Nathan Graves for your partnership and great patience with this project. May the Lord use it mightily for His purposes.

JOEL RICHARDSON

Preface

I FIRST MET NATHAN GRAVES in 2014, in what is now called the Republic of Northern Macedonia. At that time, Nathan and his wife, Lorraine, had been working in Albania for nearly twenty-one years. Nathan organized a strategic conference in the Balkans addressing the great challenges faced by the evangelical churches. I speak at a lot of conferences and in churches all over the world. This particular event was not simply impressive—it was inspired. To understand the power of what took place that year, one first needs to understand a few things about the Balkans. The Balkan Peninsula is a part of the world that most Americans know very little about. Occupying the whole of southeastern Europe, today it is comprised of around thirteen countries. Throughout this region, there are a multiplicity of ethnic, religious, and social identities—and divisions.

During the Cold War, much of this region was somewhat unified under the banner of Yugoslavia. During the 1990s a series of wars ripped the region apart. In fact, the very term Balkanize has come to refer to the breaking up of a region into smaller and more hostile units. During this period of splintering and war, more than 150,000 people died. It was also during this time that the evangelical movement began to make its first solid inroads in the area. This is when Nathan and his young family moved to the region. In a baptism by fire so to speak, they gave themselves to a place where the soil was soaked with blood and the people were deeply divided.

Although some time had passed, the painful memories of the nineties, remained. In many cases, the painful memories and divisions went back centuries. Today, there is still a tremendous amount of fear, prejudice, and division along national, ethnic, and religious lines. In some of the countries, the Muslim population is nearly 90 percent, whereas in other countries, Eastern Orthodox Christianity is dominant. Although the evangelical movement is firmly established there, they remain a minority, and are often looked at with suspicion. This is why I was so impressed with Nathan's leadership skills in organizing such a conference in that region. He had managed to gather more than two hundred prominent Christian leaders from nearly every nation in the Balkans. Even more impressive was the fact that there was nearly an equal number of Pentecostals as there were Baptists. Anyone who has been in ministry long knows that mixed denominational meetings rarely happen smoothly. Because of his commitment to the kingdom of God, however, Nathan managed to organize and pull off the impossible.

In the back of the room, several booths were set up for the many languages that were simultaneously translated throughout the conference. The few days that we gathered were among some of the most powerful, anointed, and blessed times of worship and fellowship that I have ever experienced. There was also a certain prophetic nature to the event. Among the primary purposes of the gathering was to discuss how evangelical leaders throughout the region could strategize and partner together to reach out to their Muslim neighbors and stand up to the creeping shadow of radical Islamization. I was blessed to be one of the keynote speakers and share some of the insights that I've gained by giving myself to this great challenge for the past few decades.

It was during this conference that I began to discern that Nathan would become a strategic partner in my own ministry. A year earlier I had traveled deep into the Rhodopy Mountains of Bulgaria to visit a small church that is reaching out to the many remote Muslim villages there. It was during that trip that I came to realize how strategically important the Balkans are. These fractured nations, often forgotten by many in the

West, represent the door from the Middle East to Europe. Today, there is a very real spiritual, as well as geo-political, battle for control of that tremendously important gateway. I realized then that the Balkans will play a tremendously important strategic role in the work of proclaiming the gospel to all nations before Jesus returns. Thus, it was not a shock when the very next year, Recep Tayyip Erdogan, the emerging dictator in Turkey, opened the floodgates and allowed over a million refugees from the Syrian conflict and greater Middle East to begin pouring into the Balkans toward western Europe. Largely because of the groundwork that had been laid at the conference in Macedonia, and the various networks that had developed there, many of the churches joined together and jumped at the opportunity to reach out to the hundreds of thousands of refugees who were pouring through the region.

Regardless as to how one feels about the political ramifications of the global Muslim refugee crisis, it is unarguable that followers of Jesus are called to reach out to all people. So that is exactly what they did. Among other things, they formed waypoints along the refugee road and offered to charge their phones for free. In the process, they offered to put into their phones a free micro SD cards that had been loaded with the Bible and other Christian literature in several languages. There was also contact information from churches in Europe that had expressed a desire to minister to them when they arrived. Nearly all the refugees welcomed the SD cards. Overall, it was a brilliant project. Tens of thousands of Muslims received the Bible in their language through that project.

During this period I spoke with several friends who were ministering to refugees in Germany and other European nations, and they all reported an unprecedented number of Muslims coming to faith. Of course, it is true that many faked their conversion perhaps to receive better benefits, but there is no question that a great number have genuinely come to faith over the past several years. To this day, many remain in the churches; they have been discipled and have even gone on to lead many others to the Lord. In the midst of this genuine crisis, despite its many negative ramifications, the Lord was at work.

At the heart of this book is a firm conviction that the Lord is always at work. In fact, it is specifically in the midst of catastrophe, crisis, and the times when it seems as though the Lord is most absent that He is actually most active. Learning to see gospel opportunities when many others only see crisis is not a skill that comes naturally. Yet it is a skill that the body of Christ must learn. The closer we approach the time of Jesus' return, the more natural and man-made disasters and calamities we will see. So also then will gospel opportunities increase—if we have eyes to see them. It is thus to this end and with great joy that I've joined together with Nathan to coauthor this book. It has been both a privilege and an honor. Nathan Graves is a man whose heart burns for the things that God's heart burns for and who, like the sons of Issachar, not only understands the times but also what we need to do in light of what is coming. Our mutual hope and prayer is that this book will be used to help many others fix their eyes on what God is doing in the midst of the many storms that are even now gathering on the horizon.

Part 1

A BIBLICAL THEOLOGY OF CATASTROPHE

(Nathan Graves)

"For the fleeing Albanians, their pain goes much deeper. We in the West have a hard time imagining losing our jobs. Imagine losing your home, your family pictures, the neighbors you grew up with and every possession you own. Then imagine seeing your elderly parents being beaten and forced to flee across mountains. Imagine whole families losing fathers, brothers and cousins. Imagine your five-year-old child being forced to watch the public executions of their teachers. Imagine being forced into a foreign country where you know no one except the grieving, dying people lying next to you. Imagine watching your own children dying and being able to do nothing about it. . . . Now imagine having no hope for eternity."

—KOSOVAR REFUGEE CRISIS, PERSONAL JOURNAL, MARCH 28, 1999

Introduction

IT WAS LATE, maybe around 9:30 p.m. I had just finished another long hard day of work. For the past month, since the Kosovar refugee crisis began in the spring of 1999, I was getting home around past nine and sometimes later. Soon after the flood of Kosovar Albanian refugees entered Albania, our team set up a relief and distribution center to care for their physical needs. From early morning until late at night we distributed food, clothing, and medical supplies for nearly seven hundred refugees in our area of Tirana, the capital city of Albania.

By now, I was feeling the full emotional and physical effects of the crisis. It was hard not to. Every day my family and I witnessed the trauma of people who had lost everything—their homes, their jobs, their family members and their dignity. Displaced by war and alone in a foreign country, they were hungry, grief-stricken, and exhausted.

Like many other Albanians in our neighborhood who took in refugees, those living next door to us received a family from a village near the city of Prizren in Kosovo. This family fled when the Serbian paramilitary entered their village to continue its campaign of destruction, rounding up and shooting men both young and old. After the war, I visited this village where grieving mothers and wives told us that most of the adult males were either dead or missing. Afterward they took us to a place where more than thirty men and boys were buried in a mass grave. I will never forget the unbearable stench that met us as we approached the freshly dug site.

In the panic, this household grabbed what they could and fled over the mountains into Albania. As they were fleeing, they got separated from two of the young sons and could not find them. After crossing the border, they were loaded onto an old Chinese Jiefang CA-30 army truck and transported for eight hours over some of the most unforgiving and impassable roads in Europe to the processing station in Tirana. It was there that our neighbors received them.

On my way home that evening, I rounded the corner of the road where I lived and saw a figure crouched and leaning against my gate. As I approached I could see that it was one of the refugees—a sixteen-year-old boy who was staying in the neighbor's house next to me. His head was bowed, and he was crying. I sat next to him and asked what was wrong.

Over the next several minutes, through his heartbroken sobs, he told me that his dad died. Tragically, the night before, his father was walking down one of the streets of Tirana and collapsed of a massive heart attack. While he was dying, a group of thugs robbed him of five hundred Deutsche marks, the family's remaining money. He died there on the street, having no money to leave for his wife and children. As I listened to his tragic story, I began to weep. I had nothing to say. All I could do was sit there with him and cry.

After two crisis-filled months of endlessly caring for needy and panicked refugees, I was exhausted physically and emotionally, having participated in something that went beyond anything I had known before. Up to that point, I could somewhat control my level of involvement with the nationals I was serving. Now I found myself unable to control anything around me. After seeing the daily suffering, hearing tragic stories and trying to distribute aid from sunup to sundown, I was at my whit's end. The story of this young man's father finally brought me to a point emotionally that I could not hold back the tears.

By now I had been a missionary for ten years and understood well that God uses difficult circumstances to open doors for the gospel. This was different. I was in the midst of an international crisis in which I and everyone around me felt helpless to do anything about. I wondered why God allowed this catastrophe to happen. It was more than I could bear.

Nineteen years have passed since that awful crisis in the Balkans. Since then, my family and I have witnessed and participated in other disasters in this crisis prone part of the world. The latest being the Syrian refugee crisis, in which more than a million refugees transited through the Balkans to flee the wars and fighting in Syria and Afghanistan.

When facing catastrophes of such magnitude, where homes, families and individual lives are ripped apart through war and other man-made or natural disasters, it is difficult not to ask why God allows it all to happen. So, I did. I asked God why. What I've discovered since that terrible tragedy in Kosovo is what has led me to write this book. I am grateful to be able to partner with Joel Richardson whose unique perspective I believe helps to tie together many of the ideas that the Lord placed in my heart. In our quest to understand this mystery of God's plans and purposes in catastrophe, we have discovered truths throughout the whole of Scripture that have had profound implications to our understanding of God and His global redemptive mission for the salvation of mankind. I pray that as you read this book, you will not only understand the biblical concepts that we discuss, but most importantly, catch the vision to apply these profound truths.

"When I was in the refugee camp today, my eye caught two little boys sitting alone on a bench. I went over to them and saw them crying. They were shaking and obviously very afraid. I sat between them and pulled the smaller one onto my lap. As I held him and rocked him, the tears began flowing. As he cried, his brother turned his face into my side and began sobbing. When the crying subsided, I asked the younger one his name and how old he was. His name was Bujar (which in Albanian means "generous"). He was only six. The other one's name was Fisnik (which in Albanian means "noble"). He was eight. As I held these two precious little boys, I couldn't help but think of my own two little sons who are five and eight. These could have been my own children."

—KOSOVAR REFUGEE CRISIS, PERSONAL JOURNAL, MARCH 29, 1999

BIBLICAL HISTORY OF CATASTROPHE

For the creation was subjected to futility, not willingly, but because of him who subjected it, in hope that the creation itself will be set free from its bondage to corruption.

—ROMANS 8:20-21 ESV

CATASTROPHE is a hard and sobering word that means "an event causing great and often sudden damage or suffering; a disaster." The very idea of catastrophe invokes a sense of grief and loss, but it is a word that describes much of the story of humanity. The chronology of the rise and fall of nations throughout recorded history has come as the result of the destruction, suffering and devastation caused by what we call natural and man-made disasters. From the very beginning of creation, we see God directing the movements of man on the face of the earth in the midst of catastrophe. And it is in these very catastrophes that we see the master plan of God set forth for the nations of the earth.

CAST OUT OF THE GARDEN

The first and greatest catastrophe of all time as recoded in the Bible was the fall of man. After God placed Adam in the garden, He gave him a command: "And the LORD God commanded the man, saying, 'You may surely eat of every tree of the garden, but of the tree of the knowledge of good and evil you shall not eat, for in the day you eat of it you will surely die'" (Gen. 2:16-17, NIV). We all know the story. God's prize creation, man, was made perfect, and it was only in that state of perfection that God would and could commune and fellowship with Adam and Eve. The beauty of this communion is seen when God came down to the garden to meet them and they would walk together in the coolness of the day (see Gen. 3:8). What a beautiful picture of the love of God! What bliss it must have been for both God and His creation. How Adam and Eve must have joyously awakened each morning to meet God with the sunrise and again in the approaching sunset, day after day.

We cannot miss this picture. This is what it was supposed to be like. It is what all of creation longs for once again. Imagine walking side by side with God in a stunning garden where around you all of creation is brimming with pristine beauty. Happiness abounds. Sweetness and life are deeply experienced. The childlike desire to run with the wind fills your every moment. Nothing is in conflict. You are perfectly free and perfectly at peace.

This is what Adam and Eve knew. So long as they obeyed God's one simple command, all the cares and worries of life will never be known. Then in a single instant of time, tragedy strikes and everything changes. In a moment of temptation, Adam gives in and eats of the fruit of the Tree of the Knowledge of Good and Evil and is immediately and eternally separated from God. Though the process of death began in their bodies, their spirits instantly died, and their souls were immediately separated from God. It was nothing short of sudden death.

Adam and Eve, who just moments before were scheduled to meet God for their daily walk in the garden, were now experiencing traumatic emotions—feelings they had never known before. Shame and fear overtook them, and as God called out for Adam in the garden, they tried to hide themselves and their sin by covering themselves with fig leaves sown together by their own hands.

What just occurred was a catastrophe of epic proportions. The damage and destruction caused by that one decision had a massive, global impact, never to be compared with any catastrophe to arise thereafter. The devastation was so great it permanently altered mankind and nature. All the destruction, wars, death, and tragedies of all history have come about because of this one horrendous act.

The tragedy was not just what it would mean for mankind. God, too, was permanently impacted. The loss was more deeply felt by Him than we can ever imagine. And what God would have to do to ever restore Adam and the rest of mankind back to Himself would require an act on the part of God so incredibly unbelievable, the catastrophe of the fall could never compare to the one God Himself would experience when He would one day send man's Deliverer.

This plan of restoring Adam and Eve and all of creation was set in motion immediately. The first promise of the coming Redeemer was given in Genesis 3:15, which states that one day the Deliverer would crush the head of Satan the serpent. Then, rather than accepting the coverings they made for themselves, God killed an animal and clothed Adam and Eve with the skins. This was a foreshadow of the ultimate sacrifice that would one day be made to wipe away the sins of the world so that we may be clothed with His righteousness.

Next, God casts Adam and Eve out of the garden:

> Then the LORD God said, "Behold, the man has become like one of us in knowing good and evil. Now, lest he reach out his hand and take also of the tree of life and eat, and live forever"—therefore the LORD God sent him out of the garden of Eden to work the ground from which he was taken. He drove out the man, and at the east of the garden he placed the cherubim and a flaming sword that turned every way to guard the way to the tree of life. (Gen. 3.22-24, NIV)

This is the first case of human displacement we see in history. Adam and Eve were in the garden and God cast them out. More than that, He forcefully removed them from their homes and all that was familiar to them. If we consider the definition of a refugee—"A person who has been forced to leave their country in order to escape war, persecution, or natural disaster"—Adam and Eve can be viewed as humanity's first refugees. In their case, they were forced out, not because of some horrible thing done to them, but because of something terrible they had done to themselves.

God's forcefully moving Adam and Eve out of the garden of Eden set forth a pattern of forced displacement of people by God that we see in the whole narrative of Scripture. It all has to do with His global plan for His glory and the redemption of mankind. Had God not cast Adam and Eve out of the garden and placed the cherubim at the entrance to keep them from returning, they would have eaten from the Tree of Life and lived forever in a lost state of sin and separation from God. What a tragedy it would have indeed been had they lived in this perpetual state. God drove them out to save them. He had to bring about a traumatic crisis in Adam and Eve's lives to prevent them from doing eternal harm to their souls and to the whole of mankind that would proceed from them.

THE FLOOD

Adam's sin was passed down to his children and his children's children until humanity was overcome with wickedness. The Bible says:

> The Lord saw how great the wickedness of the human race had become on the earth, and that every inclination of the thoughts of the human heart was only evil all the time. The Lord regretted that he had made human beings on the earth, and his heart was deeply troubled. So, the Lord said, "I will wipe from the face of the earth the human race I have created—and with them the animals, the birds and the creatures that move along the ground—for I regret that I have made them. But Noah found favor in the eyes of the Lord. (Genesis 6:5-8, NIV)

We need to stop here for a moment and ask ourselves, "Does God bring destruction and calamity? Does our loving and gracious God cause disasters to occur in the world?" Read these words God spoke to Noah: "I have determined to make an end of all flesh for the earth is filled with violence through them. Behold I will destroy them with the earth" (Gen. 6:13, ESV).

A massive "natural disaster" orchestrated by God wiped out the earth and all its inhabitants. The earth did not destroy itself. God destroyed it. He destroyed the animals, the birds, all the creatures that moved along the ground and all of humanity, except for Noah and his family and the animals they brought on the ark. Why? Had God not destroyed the world, the world would have destroyed itself and the line of the coming Deliverer would have been altogether corrupted. God destroyed that He might save. God brought calamity to his beloved world so that one day it might see the fulfillment of His divine plan to save it. God saved Noah and his family to preserve the line of the coming Redeemer.

Though Noah was a righteous man, he and his family experienced the full weight of this global catastrophe. When the flood came, the waters lifted the ark from the face of the earth and carried them for 150 days until it rested on a mountain far away from where he once lived. Displaced and separated from all they knew, Noah and his family had to begin a new life, alone in the world.

THE TOWER OF BABEL

After the flood, it didn't take long for mankind to once again fill the earth with its evil ways. The great catastrophe of sin brought about by Adam was not settled by the great flood brought about by God. The sin continued through Noah, his wife, and his children. Then in Genesis 10 we see the Table of Nations. From the sons of Noah, we see all the nations of the world speaking the same language and migrating together into one place in the land of Shinar.

This was in direct disobedience to God's command given to Noah and his sons: "As for you, be fruitful and increase in number; multiply on the earth and increase upon it" (Gen. 9:7, NIV). This was the second time God gave the command to be fruitful and multiply and fill the earth. He had also given the command to Adam in Genesis 1:28. This command is directly and essentially linked to God's redemptive plan for the world as we shall see.

But it is never the goal or desire of corrupted man to do the will of God. Our nature is to follow selfish pursuits. Our intentions are to turn inward to what is familiar and safe. Our driving ambition is to guard the things we love and to maintain our personal, physical security. Our nature is to build fortresses and compounds, to protect our interests, and to make names for ourselves. We will protect our little kingdoms regardless of what God may command or what He may want. These were the desires of the people of Shinar, and these have been the interests of all mankind since the beginning of time. Because of this, God must step in. Let's consider the account:

> They said to one another, "Come, let us make bricks and burn them thoroughly." And they used brick for stone, and they used tar for mortar. They said, "Come, let us build for ourselves a city, and a tower whose top will reach into heaven, and let us make for ourselves a name, otherwise we will be scattered abroad over the face of the whole earth." (Genesis 11:3-4)

The people said they would build for themselves a city, and they would make a name for themselves in defiance to God's command to fill the earth. Once again, we see a disaster, brought about by God, causing mass migration and displacement of people. God confounded the languages so that the people would have no other choice than to separate and move away from one another to the East, West, North, and South. It was a refugee crisis on an unheard-of scale.

ABRAHAM CALLED TO LEAVE

Once man was scattering over the earth, God continued to implement his plan to bring reconciliation to the world and to make his name known throughout the earth by way of catastrophe. Again, we see the workings of God in migration and displacement through the life of Abraham. "The LORD had said to Abram, 'Go from your country, your people and your father's household to the land I will show you'" (Gen. 12:1, NIV).

This verse is revealing in its description of what all refugees experience. When they flee, they leave behind everything important to them: their country, their people, and their family. Having lived in an Eastern culture for nearly a quarter century, it cannot be overstated how important these things are, especially family. For many Westerners, the task is often prioritized over other things. For Easterners, the family trumps all. The idea of leaving behind one's family is unthinkable. This is why when most Easterners migrate, they will do all they can to bring their family members with them, or what we would refer to as chain migration.

Yet for Abraham, God was calling him to separate himself not only from his extended family, but from his ethnicity and his nationality as well. It was a call that must have brought great anxiety to Abraham and deep sorrow to everyone close to him. Much could be said about this and probably should. The sadness and lack of understanding by family undoubtedly was profound and none can identify more with these sorrows than the Lord Himself.

Here again we see God shifting individuals from one geographic point to another in order to fulfill His redemptive plan for the world. This calling out of Abraham to leave his country and go to a place God would show him was specifically tied to God's plan for the nations of the earth. In the following verses we read, "I will make you into a great nation, and I will bless you; I will make your name great, and you will be a blessing. I will bless those who bless you, and whoever curses you I will curse; and all peoples on earth will be blessed through you" (Gen. 12:2-3, NIV).

This promise that all the peoples of the world would be blessed through Abraham was another prophecy regarding the promised Deliverer who would one day come and bear the sins of the world. This Deliverer would one day bless every nation—every tribe and tongue and people—on the earth with forgiveness of sins and eternal life. Through this coming Redeemer, mankind and all of creation would one day be restored back to God. The geographic location where all of this would be centered required Abraham to leave on a long and arduous migration to the promise land.

The call to Abraham was to leave and to follow God wherever He led him. Why couldn't God have fulfilled His plan right where Abraham was? Why couldn't God have made it easy on Abraham and let him stay in Ur of the Chaldees? Because the plans and purposes of God for mankind can only be fulfilled when God does things His way. There are no short cuts. In the sovereign strategy of God, He moves people whenever and wherever He wills to fulfill those plans and purposes. Abraham had to leave. There was no other way. Abraham's act of great personal sacrifice to leave everything was among his greatest acts of faith.

JOSEPH SOLD AS A SLAVE

Between the time Abraham and Lot arrived in Canaan and when Joseph was bought into slavery in Egypt, there were a series of crises, disasters, and catastrophes, leading to fleeing and migration. From Abram and Sarai's flight to Egypt because of the severe famine in the land to Lot escaping the destruction of Sodom to Hagar being sent off into the wilderness with Ishmael to Jacob fleeing from Esau back to Ur and then fleeing from Laban back again to Canaan the pattern of the migration of people due to catastrophe is abundant and clear.

God causes catastrophe to reveal His divine purposes of love and grace, not just for Israel and the church, but for all people. The story of Joseph is particularly poignant in revealing this truth. Joseph's words to his brothers in Genesis say it all: "It was not you who sent me here, but God" (Gen. 45:8). How often in our own personal lives do we despair when tragedy strikes? We automatically think, "This cannot be from God. He would never cause or allow such awful things to happen to me!" We equate the goodness of God with good circumstances. When bad things happen, we automatically assume they are always the result of Satan. But Scripture shows us otherwise.

Left to ourselves, we will usually choose what is contrary to the will of God for ourselves and others. It is the nature of man. But even when we choose to do God's will, we may very well be struck and even targeted for crisis. The reason goes beyond what He wants to accomplish in us personally. It is also because we are a part of this unfolding mystery of God to save the world and to fill it with His glory. For this reason, He uses whomever He wills. Sometimes the very ones who endure the most hardship and severe testing are the ones most near and dear to the heart of God. It is because they are the faithful ones who can be entrusted with suffering, which in turn brings about a greater deliverance. That was what happened with Joseph.

When Joseph was thrown into the pit by his jealous and angry brothers, we can only wonder what he must have thought. After bragging about his dreams of one day ruling over his parents and brothers, Joseph must have been filled with remorse and regret for his arrogance. Though the Scriptures do not tell us, undoubtedly Joseph must have wondered if he would live through his ordeal. Then when he was pulled from the well and sold to a caravan of merchants traveling to Egypt, the reality of it all must have hit him like a ton of bricks. When catastrophe strikes, there is usually little warning. What greater catastrophe could Joseph have endured than to lose everything most precious to him, and be betrayed by his brothers, only to become an exile and slave in the land of Egypt?

While in Egypt, serving time in prison for a crime he didn't commit, Joseph was called to interpret a dream of Pharaoh. In that dream, it was revealed that there would be seven years of plenty in the land followed by seven years of famine. In the seven years of plenty, Joseph, who became second in command in the land of Egypt, stored food during the time of plenty in preparation for the time of famine to come. This drove the sons of Israel into Egypt to buy food, without which they would have died.

God brought a personal disaster directly to Joseph so that Joseph would be His tool for saving many from utter ruin in a global, natural disaster. Among those who were saved were two groups of people. The first people who were saved were the Hebrews, in order preserve the line of the coming Deliverer. Joseph said to his brothers: "And God sent me before you to preserve for you a remnant on earth, and to keep alive for you many survivors" (Gen. 45:7, ESV). The second group were the nations of the earth: "As for you, you meant evil against me, but God meant it for good, to bring it about that many people should be kept alive, as they are today" (Gen. 50:20, ESV).

It is a paradox that can be understood only when we comprehend God's nature as opposed to our nature. We simply do not understand how infinitely good God is. Nor do we grasp the depth of the evil in the heart of man. God does not partner with the world in order to make His ways known. The world system is opposed to God, and God is opposed to it. In this cosmic opposition, the plans of God prevail in the world, and the world submits only when it sees that it cannot stand against Him. When catastrophes overtake people's lives, they are humbled by their losses and weakness. It is then they will cry out to the God who cares: "Yet does not one in a heap of ruins stretch out his hand, and in his disaster cry for help?" (Job 30:24, ESV).

This shuffling and reshuffling of people as migrants and refugees from region to region and from nation to nation through war, famine, slavery, regional and global destruction, is all playing an important part in the unfolding plan of God to the ends of the earth. What we have seen to this point in time continues on in the Old Testament, into the New, extending into this present hour. All of these disasters will continue to intensify until the day comes when the last nations on earth stretch forth their hands and cry out to receive salvation in Jesus Christ.

THE PLAGUES OF EGYPT

God kept His promise in keeping many Hebrews alive—in Egypt that is. Displaced in a foreign country for 430 years, God increased their numbers in great measure. God had not forgotten his oath to Abraham to make his descendants as numerous as the sand of the sea and bless every nation on earth through him. God was right on track.

The road to fulfilling God's plan to send the promised Deliverer had been paved by tragedy, ruin and destruction. Time and again, these calamities had caused widespread refugee crises, immense human suffering, slavery, and total devastation to homes and families.

The ten plagues that fell on the land of Egypt came by the hand of God. Pharaoh's refusal to let God's children go resulted in the total destruction of Egypt. But we should also consider that the children of Israel might not have been so inclined themselves to commit to such a mass migration back to Canaan if they had not witnessed the destruction themselves. They said to Moses just six weeks after leaving Egypt when they were hungry and in the desert: "If only we had died by the Lord's hand in Egypt! There we sat around pots of meat and ate all the food we wanted, but you brought us out into this desert to starve this entire assembly to death!" (Ex. 16:3, NIV).

Here again we see this conflict between the interests of God in the salvation of Israel and mankind, and the selfish interests of man in his petty and worldly pursuits. Just as the people of Shinar wanted to hold onto life as they knew and wanted it, resulting in the destruction of their Babylonian civilization, so the people of Israel would have stayed in the land of Egypt as long as their stomachs were filled, and they were left alone by the Egyptians. Had this happened the stage would have never been set for the Savior of the world, the Lamb of God to come and bear the sin of the world.

Before the last disaster fell, which would kill the firstborn of all Egyptian families, God instructed Moses what the Israelites needed to do to be spared the destruction. The sacrificial lamb slain by the head of each home had to be prepared and sacrificed exactly as God instructed. Then when the Lord would pass through the land of Egypt and see the blood of the lamb on the lintel (the top) and the two doorposts (the sides)—representing the cross—He would pass over the home and not allow the destroyer to smite them.

In this Passover sacrifice, God made it clear to Israel what He would do one day to reconcile the world back to Himself. Sometimes God has to bring catastrophe to pry man away from his goals for himself so that the Lord's goals will be accomplished to fill the earth with His glory in the salvation of all nations. As we are seeing, because we live in a sin-cursed world, where men are opposed to God, it takes overwhelming catastrophes on a national and global scale to accomplish this.

JOB'S CATASTROPHE

Next to the flood, the catastrophe which befell Job is probably the best known in the Bible. Is it also just as well known that it was God who initiated the catastrophe? It wasn't the devil who came to God asking if he could annihilate Job's family, bring him to absolute economic ruin and attack his body with unbearable pain. It was God who said to Satan, "Have you considered My servant Job?" (Job 1:8). Consider what about him? What would God want the devil to consider regarding Job? Satan did not even mention Job's name. Job's suffering was initiated and caused by God but inflicted by Satan. Why?

As I have read and studied the book of Job over the years, my appreciation of its meaning has grown immensely. Imagine Job lying in the open air at night. The winds of the Middle East are whistling across the desert sands. The surroundings are mysterious, almost surreal. Sounds can be heard everywhere: from his three judging friends and one compassionate friend (Elihu), from Job's own groans of intense pain, and from the sounds of the swirling whirlwind of the night. Mingled with the noise is a deeply felt presence of a multitude of peering eyes. Looking from all directions is the concentrated gaze from the eyes of seen and unseen faces: the faces of earth, of heaven, and of hell. All of creation is focused on Job, asking one question: "What is God's purpose in all of this suffering?"

In Job's solemn reflection of better times, at the height of human success when he helped the helpless and lived a model life of goodness to others, he declared what his own reward should have been when he said, 'I shall die in my nest, and I shall multiply my days as the sand'" (Job 29:18). Job loved God and he served others, but he also loved himself and determined what his reward for his own justice and his own integrity should be. Then, without warning, Job was bedridden in unbearable pain, hearing the scorn of those closest to him. He had nothing to show for his good life. His soft, secure nest was gone.

Is Job's story so different than our own? It's unlikely any of us have suffered to the degree Job has. Yet it doesn't take long to recognize striking similarities between how Job understood his purpose in life and how we see our own as we journey through this world. Job believed he was a good man and had served God faithfully. Because of this, he felt that God was unjust to bring such suffering to him (see Job 9:22-24). If Job could have determined his reward for all the good he'd done, it would be to live long and to retire in his nice, comfortable, and secure nest.

Now the question we might ask is, "Was that too much for Job to ask?" Maybe not. Job was a good and righteous man, but nests are made to be born in, not to die in. Some of the mystery of Job's suffering possibly can be answered by looking into God's dealings in our own lives. Elihu said to Job, "For God speaks once, yea twice, yet man perceives it not...Lo, all these things God works oftentimes with man, to bring back his soul from the pit, to be enlightened with the light of the living" (Job 33:14, 29-30).

What nests are we building today with the view that one day they will bring us the security and happiness we need? What nests are we constructing for ourselves because we feel we somehow deserve them for all the good, hard work we have done? We've lived in such a way, worked in such a way, or served in such a way that we may think it's our turn now to live out our days in peace and die in our nests of ease.

As sojourners in this present world, God never intended for us to live or to die this way. If we build our nests to die in, we've missed the purpose for which God has placed us in this world. God wasn't finished with Job. His work was not done. God wanted to determine Job's reward at the end of his life. The nest in which Job envisioned dying was not what God had in mind at all, though God later restored everything to him. So, too, it is for each of us. Though weary and worn in well doing, the prize for the fight is not found in this world, and we are never to look for it here. God is preparing us a nest, a resting place where all trials and burdens will cease. But until then we are to soar above the enticing nests below with an understanding that one day our lives here will be over and all that will matter in the end is that we gave our all for Him.

THE DIASPORA OF THE EARLY CHURCH

We could continue with more examples in the Old Testament of how God scatters people through catastrophe, including the Assyrian and Babylonian captivities. But let's move on to the New Testament and see that this pattern of God in the displacement and migration of people through catastrophe continues even into the age of grace.

After Jesus' resurrection, He said to his disciples, "But you will receive power when the Holy Spirit comes upon you, and you will be my witnesses in Jerusalem and in all Judea and Samaria, and to the ends of the earth" (Acts 1:8, ESV). This command was all inclusive and was to be done simultaneously. Jesus didn't say to begin this work "*first* in Jerusalem, *then* in all Judea." He said, "In Jerusalem *and* in all Judea *and* Samaria, *and* to the ends of the earth."

Jesus was not telling these disciples that He wanted them to begin only in Jerusalem and finish the job there before moving on to Judea and Samaria, then to the rest of the world. He was telling them to go into all the world—*all of it at the same time*—now. It was not a first-then mandate. It was a both-and mandate. Jesus placed the responsibility for evangelizing the entire world squarely on their shoulders.

This is significant in light of the selfish purpose and nature of man for himself compared to the divine purpose and nature of God for the world. These natures are always in conflict. If man is given the option to stay where he is most at home—with family, friends, homes, comforts and all things familiar—he will take it. It is rare to find those who will intentionally leave all they know and love to venture into the unknown, to live and work in strange and difficult environments for eternal purposes. This pattern of God's people stubbornly putting their roots deep into this world, clinging to all they hold dear in this life has been one of the greatest obstacles for completing the Great Commission and filling the earth with the glory of the Lord.

Because this is true, God *must* bring catastrophe even to his beloved church. Had the early disciples not experienced severe persecution, it is unlikely that many would have ever ventured far beyond the gates of Jerusalem with the message of salvation. The spirit of Shinar is not far from any of us. Although the Holy Spirit indwells the believer, the flesh is still resident. With every opportunity to oppose God, the flesh rises up within us to do battle with God's plans and purposes. The flesh, that part of us that the Apostle Paul found difficult to describe, is ever present and must be annihilated. If not, this sinister monster will rob us of all our spiritual strength and keep us from being effective for God. So to strengthen, purify, and embolden the early believers to be his witnesses, and to keep them trusting in Him, God brought a great persecution to the church: "And there arose on that day a great persecution against the church in Jerusalem, and they were all scattered throughout the regions of Judea and Samaria, except the apostles" (Acts 8:1, ESV).

We see here that God made sure his both-and mandate for Judea *and* Samaria began. By bringing a disaster to the body of Christ, He made certain that the church scattered as refugees from Jerusalem into these locations: "Now those who were scattered went about preaching the word. Philip went down to the city of Samaria and proclaimed to them the Christ" (Acts 8:4-5, ESV). The persecution then took the disciples beyond Judea and Samaria to further parts of the earth: "Now those who were scattered because of the persecution that arose over Stephen traveled as far as Phoenicia and Cyprus and Antioch, speaking the word to no one except Jews" (Acts 11:19, ESV).

This scattering of the church had a two-fold purpose. First, it forced them out of their secure nest and into the larger world with the gospel message. Second, it reminded Christ's followers that they will never be citizens of this world: "For our citizenship is in heaven, from which also we eagerly wait for a Savior, the Lord Jesus Christ" (Phil 3:20).

If God remains consistent in how he has acted throughout history, we should understand that God will continue to bring about catastrophe to the world and to the church. The reason is that the remaining task of completing the Great Commission is not yet complete. Second, we are pilgrims on our journey to heaven, and we need to be continuously reminded that this present world is not our home.

"*I saw a young man walking alone with an elderly woman clinging to his arm. He was weighed down with their belongings. I approached and asked if I could carry something for him? He kindly refused, but later allowed me to carry his mother's hand bag. I asked him where they were from and why they were leaving. He began telling me a detailed story of his city in Syria of two million people that had been bombed, and how nearly everyone had fled. . . . I could see that not too far ahead I was going to have to leave him. . . . I asked, "Will you allow me to pray for you and your mother in the name of Jesus?" He smiled and said yes. So I prayed, asking God to give them safety on their journey and to help them. I prayed for their eyes to be opened and then ended my prayer in Jesus name.*"

—SYRIAN REFUGEE CRISIS PERSONAL JOURNAL, OCTOBER 10, 2015

HIS WAY IS IN THE WHIRLWIND

The LORD is slow to anger but great in power; the LORD will not leave the guilty unpunished. His way is in the whirlwind and the storm, and clouds are the dust of his feet"

—NAHUM 1:3

THE NOTION THAT God would ever do anything that would cause harm to another is anathema to most people. In this Laodicean age where human rights have become the manifesto of a new global, humanist religion, there is no room for the God of the Bible, especially a God who would cause harm. It is a mantra even the church has picked up on and run wild with. Aren't we supposed to have our best lives now? Actually, no.

The Bible declares that we are foreigners and exiles in this world (see 1 Pet. 2:11; John 15:18-19; Phil 3:20; Heb. 11:13-16). As such, we should expect to experience what foreigners and exiles experience. It is not an easy life for the spiritual refugee any more than it is for the physical one. They are displaced people, and so are we. If there were ever a people in this world we should be able to identify with, it is the foreigner and refugee. If there were ever a people Christians should be able to understand, it is the displaced exile. They are living in a distant land and suffering the reproaches of a foreign people just like us.

God understands this better than any of us. He is not oblivious to the plight of the physical refugee, just as He is not to ours. His heart is touched by their grief and pain. He hears their anguished cries and sees their downcast faces. He looks on them with deep and caring compassion. His desire is to bring healing to their wounds and to rescue them from their sorrows. His ear is attentive to their slightest cry and is ready to receive them with outstretched arms at their smallest movement toward him. It is for this purpose that he wounds and strikes and tears to pieces. He does so that he might heal and rescue and give life.

> See now that I myself am He! There is no god besides me. I put to death and I bring life, I have wounded and I heal, and no one can deliver out of my hand. (Deuteronomy 32:39, NIV)

> The LORD will strike Egypt with a plague; he will strike them and he will heal them. They will turn to the LORD, and he will respond to their pleas and heal them. (Isaiah 19:22, NIV)

> Come, let us return to the LORD. He has torn us to pieces but he will heal us; he has injured us but he will bind up our wounds." (Hosea 6:1, NIV)

The Lord strikes, then heals. He injures, then binds up the very wounds He inflicts. He tears to pieces, then restores to health. He puts to death, then gives life. It is a perfect paradox. God does the thing that makes no sense—the opposite of our logical perspective. Humanly speaking, it is a mystery too difficult to understand, a contradiction to common sense, an illogical display of all we think about God. Regardless of how harsh or fallacious this all may seem, it is altogether true.

As creatures living in time and space, our perspective is limited. Our abilities to perceive truth and reality can take us only so far. This is why without faith it is impossible to please God. When things don't make sense to us, we simply have to believe Him at His word. As created beings, we cannot fully perceive the Creator God who is altogether different than us, and whose ways are altogether different than ours.

In order for it all to make sense to us, we would need to be living, seeing and perceiving a multi-dimensional reality in the same way God does. But in our sinful state we cannot. And when we conclude that God must somehow see it our way, or do things that make sense to us, then we have diminished a thrice holy God, to a miniature, limited being like ourselves. Yet, in our weaknesses, God still gives us vivid glimpses of His nature and His ways.

WOUNDING TO BEAR FRUIT

Isaiah tells us that "the Lord binds up the brokenness of his people, and heals the wounds inflicted by his blow" (Isaiah 30:26, ESV). Although this is a hard thing for us to consider, this striking, wounding, and inflicting by God in order to heal and produce life is perfectly consistent with the natural world He created. A number of plants and trees need fire to survive and germinate. The seeds of the great redwoods of California remain in their cones until they are released by the heat of forest fires. The lodgepole pine, Eucalyptus, and Banksia, and other plants all depend on fires for their survival.[1]

In the Mediterranean environment of the Balkans, grapes are a plenteous commodity. The tending of grape vines in this region is as second nature to Greeks and Albanians as shoveling snow is for Canadians. One day we asked our landlord how we could have more leaves to give us more privacy in our courtyard. He said just let them grow and don't prune them. The product was more leaves but almost no fruit.

Jesus Himself uses the example of cutting or pruning vines to produce more fruit as an example of what God does in our lives. He depicts the Father as the vinedresser. He inflicts wounds that in Him we might bear much fruit: "I am the true vine, and my Father is the vinedresser. Every branch in me that does not bear fruit he takes away, and every branch that does bear fruit he prunes, that it may bear more fruit" (John 15:1-2, NIV).

THE GOD WHO BRINGS CATASTROPHE

It is clear God brings catastrophe. God causes crisis, orders destruction, and creates disaster. The same God who magnificently designed and made the earth is the same God who destroys it. The Lord who prospers the ways of man one day is the same Lord who brings him to financial ruin the next. The very God who formed man from the dust of the ground and breathed life into his nostrils is the same God who strikes him with suffering and misery and puts him to death. Crush a mature dandelion and watch the wind carry off the seeds. God crushes the nations to scatter the peoples across the earth that His life may be born in the hearts of many:

> I form the light and create darkness, I bring prosperity and create disaster; I, the LORD, do all these things. (Isaiah 45:7, NIV)

> When a trumpet sounds in a city, do not the people tremble? When disaster comes to a city, has not the LORD caused it? (Amos 3:6)

Though it goes against all our culturally or even our theologically shaped reasoning, we must accept and embrace this hard truth if we are going to better understand God and His ways. If we want to have wisdom and insight about our role in bringing about salvation and the glory of God to the nations, we have to allow God to reshape our understanding of who He is and what He is doing in His world. His ways are not only declared to be in the stillness and serene (see Psalm 46:10). Much more so, they are also to be found in the whirlwind and the storm:

> The LORD answered Job out of the whirlwind. (Job 38:1)

> You will be visited by the LORD of hosts with thunder and with earthquake and great noise, with whirlwind and tempest, and the flame of a devouring fire. (Isaiah 29:6, ESV)

> I scattered them with a whirlwind among all the nations that they had not known. Thus the land they left was desolate, so that no one went to and fro, and the pleasant land was made desolate. (Zechariah 7:14, ESV)

And the LORD will cause his majestic voice to be heard and the descending blow of his arm to be seen, in furious anger and a flame of devouring fire, with a cloudburst and storm and hailstones. (Isaiah 30:30, ESV)

It really comes down to two fundamental truths: God is holy and men are sinful. God loves man, but man hates God. So we see that when God purposefully brings catastrophe, it is not because He is unjust, and man is a victim. It is because of man's very rejection of God that He must bring about not just hardship but large-scale calamity to turn man's heart to him. How often do we see this in life? Whenever we determine to go our own way, as opposed to God's way, and do what is right in our own eyes, pinpricks don't help much in turning us around. We quickly forget and continue on doing what we want. God clarifies this truth in Chronicles:

When I shut up the heavens so that there is no rain, or command the locust to devour the land, or send pestilence among my people, if my people who are called by my name humble themselves, and pray and seek my face and turn from their wicked ways, then I will hear from heaven and will forgive their sin and heal their land. (2 Chronicles 7:13-14, ESV)

In this passage we see God's ways in full view. He brings drought, locusts, and pestilence to His own people, so they will repent. Then when his people humble themselves, pray, and seek His face, He heals them from the very torments He brings. His way is in the whirlwind and the storm.

If God will do such a thing to his own people, He will certainly do the same, if not more, to those who are outside his fold, in order to bring them in. It is *because* God is love that He inflicts hardships. It is *because* God wants people to be saved that he scatters them. The evil rulers of this world are not at all inclined to open their borders or airwaves to the message of the Bible that their people may hear truth. So God must bring disaster. Catastrophe is the conduit through which God's command to fill the earth is enforced upon the nations, and through which he gives opportunity for them to repent.

If God did not spare his own Son, but gave Himself up for us all (see Rom. 8:32), then to what lengths will God not go to save those who are far away? If God loves the world and sent his Son to die for the world (see John 3:16), then we should expect that He will make a way for people to hear. Throughout history, we see God's primary method for waking up the nations to repentance is through man-made and natural disasters. And if God's primary method for bringing lost people into the path of His people is through such catastrophes, then it only makes sense that we should expect He will bring disasters to those nations who are holding the doors closed to the gospel.

This is exactly what we are seeing today in much of the Muslim world, from Afghanistan to Iraq to Syria and to much of North Africa. The present-day regional conflicts, wars, and natural disasters are clear indicators that God is at work in these places to open the doors for people to flee or for Christians to enter. God is causing disaster to befall Muslim nations, not as acts of judgments necessarily, but as a means of penetrating the barriers established by evil empires and kings. He is afflicting them with war and natural disasters and tearing them to pieces by sectarian violence that they may find their way to Him and discover true peace, rest, and healing for their souls.

GOD'S COMMAND TO FILL THE EARTH

Throughout history, man has ruled the nations of the earth. Mighty kings and rulers have arisen to extend their kingdoms farther and farther across the globe. To garner more power, to have more riches and land is the insatiable desire of fallen man. The purpose of kings has been to shape the world in their image, to make a name for themselves, and ultimately to have the power of the gods.

Countless millions have died because of wars waged by those who "want it all" and who will stop at nothing to conquer the world. These advancing armies of history have left catastrophic destruction in their wake in order to have nothing less than total global dominion. Each time, though it was God who raised them up, He limited how far they could go because that dominion belongs only to one person. His name is Jesus Christ. Man's rule on earth is limited and in the power of sin. Christ's future rule is infinite and with the scepter of righteousness.

One day King Jesus will reign on the earth—the whole earth. In that day, he will take the power from all nations and kings and set up His kingdom, an everlasting kingdom where His righteousness will prevail globally, and He will rule with a rod of iron. His glory will be spread from sea to sea and all peoples will know and worship Him as the absolute sovereign of this world:

All the nations that you have made will come and worship before you, Lord; they will bring glory to your name. (Psalm 86:9, NIV)

All the ends of the earth shall remember and turn to the Lord, and all the families of the nations shall worship before you. (Psalm 22:27, ESV)

As salvation increases to all nations and all families of nations across the globe, the glory and thanksgiving given to God will also increase. The more that are saved, the louder the anthem of praise to our God will be. "For it is all for your sake, so that as grace extends to more and more people it may increase thanksgiving to the glory of God" (2 Cor. 4:15, ESV).

A day is coming when the whole earth will be filled with the knowledge of the Lord. It was a prayer and hope expressed by the prophets. It was a prophecy that will come to pass as sure as the sun will rise tomorrow. Though they do not know it is Him, the future rule and reign of Jesus is the desire of all nations, and He will come one day to fulfill their desire: "I will shake all nations, and the One desired by all nations will come. Then I will fill this house with glory, says the Lord of the Heavenly Armies" (Hag. 2:7, ISV).

Jesus Christ will be given an earthly kingdom where He will sit on the throne of David from which He will rule the entire world (see Luke

1:32). The spiritual kingdom, or the rule of God, is in each follower of Jesus Christ. But there will also come a day when a physical kingdom of God will be established, where Jesus will physically rule and reign from Israel. This is the ultimate goal and the grand prize that will be given to Jesus Christ by His Father as we shall later see. The ultimate plan of God for worldwide peace, which will be instituted by the Prince of Peace, is playing out step by step by way of worldwide catastrophe. What a glorious truth! But the Good News of the kingdom is only good to those who have accepted the Good News of the saving power of the death and resurrection of Jesus Christ.

THE BIBLICAL WORLDVIEW

The Bible is a story, a narrative of God from the beginning of earth's founding and fall to its final conclusion and grand climax of God's amazing victory over all of His foes. It is a total worldview system. Every worldview is a story. It has a beginning, a plot, and a final conclusion. For example, in evolution, we are falsely told life began with a single cell in some cosmic soup. Over vast periods of time, life went from a single cell and evolved into advanced forms of life we see today—and will continue to advance so long as life continues.

Worldviews give meaning to people. They tell them where they came from, where they are now, and what will be their final destination. They are not fragmented pieces of information thrown together randomly. They tell a complete narrative and give meaning to life. The devil has cleverly devised many substitute worldviews to challenge the story of God to give people a false sense of meaning and purpose. God wants to rescue them from those false systems, so they can know Him and participate in the real, true story of their history and future from God's perspective.

God's story will be completely told. There was a beginning, there is a plot, and there will be a conclusion. We are not just going to drift off into an eternal state. There is coming a day when all of history will meet with God in a grand climax on this earth, and this climax will come on the heels of the Great Tribulation. Then He will be recognized by all people as the sovereign King of the world, and His glory will be fully brought in and celebrated among all peoples, kindreds, tongues, and nations.

This story of humanity has been, is being, and will be written in catastrophe. The idealized world in which we live today, that hopes and dreams for a world without violence and war, will not come until all things once again are under the full and eternal control of the sovereign reign of the King of kings and Lord of lords. Until that day, the biblical narrative will continue to prove that catastrophe is the primary means by which God will fulfill his worldwide redemptive plan. Because this is the case, we will continue to see global disasters, causing large scale migration and displacement of peoples among the nations. So long as unredeemed man builds his Babylonian towers of defiance and resistance against the Lord, calamity, leading to the strewing of peoples as refugees and exiles over the face of the earth, will fall from the Lord of Hosts.

If we are going to fully grasp our role in the salvation of the nations, this is the lens through which we must see our story and the story of humanity. It is the reality given to us from the Bible. Throughout the narrative of Scripture, we see the central role that catastrophe has taken, is taking, and will take to completely tell the full account of God.

*"'And he [Jonah] prayed to the L*ORD *and said, "O L*ORD*, is this not what I said when I was yet in my country? That is why I made haste to flee to Tarshish; for I knew that you are a gracious God and merciful, slow to anger and abounding in steadfast love, and relenting from disaster"' (Jonah 4:2). Due to the war and the ruthless occupation of the city, the nearly 750,000 people of Mosul (Nineveh) are in desperate need. Besides the torment of their oppressors, many of them are fleeing due to lack of food, drinking water, and electricity. A large number of those fleeing are widows and children. Isn't it ironic that Jonah, when God called him to go and preach to the same city, didn't flee from God because he was afraid of going. He fled because he selfishly did not want the wicked people of Nineveh to experience the goodness and kindness of God. He despised the Ninevites and knew that if he went and preached, God would be gracious and pour out His mercy on them. Jonah's hatred for this people—the evil Assyrians—was so great that he was willing to be thrown overboard and die rather than to see these Gentile people saved and kept from disaster. Sound familiar? Not much has changed since the time of Jonah. The difference today is that (in this case) instead of God sending a Jew to preach repentance to his Assyrian oppressors in Nineveh, He is sending Christians to preach the gospel to our Muslim oppressors in Mosul. What hasn't changed is that we, like Jonah, flee from preaching peace to those who seek to do us harm, while the whole time God is going to great lengths to direct us there to save them. 'And the L*ORD *said, "You pity the plant, for which you did not labor nor did you make it grow, which came into being in a night and perished in a night. And should I not pity Nineveh, that great city, in which there are more than 120,000 persons who do not know their right hand from their left?" (Jonah 4:10-11).'"*

—PERSONAL JOURNAL, MARCH 24, 2017

3

THE MYSTERY OF CATASTROPHE

He reveals what is profoundly mysterious and knows what is in the darkness; with him dwells light.

—DANIEL 2:22

IN THE BIBLE, a mystery may refer to something that was previously concealed but has now been revealed. When the Apostle Paul speaks of the mystery of Christ in Ephesians 3:3-6, he refers to the gentiles being given the rights of inheritance and membership in the body of Christ. This truth was hidden in the ages past but was revealed to the apostles and prophets by the Spirit.

God revealed to Daniel a great deal about the future, but not everything. There were things he sought to understand but was not permitted to know. God told Daniel to "shut up the words and seal the book, until the time of the end. Many shall run to and fro, and knowledge shall increase" (Dan. 12:4, ESV). Though the full revelation of this prophecy would not be given to Daniel, in time the mystery would be understood by others at the time of the end.

The mystery of catastrophe, on the other hand, is not shut up. It is in plain view throughout the Bible. Part of the mystery is really how we have missed it. We have known about the diaspora of Israel, other peoples and nations, and the early church. The mystery of catastrophe discloses a fuller and deeper understanding of the *why* and the *what* behind diaspora and the catastrophes which lead to movements of people as refugees, migrants, and displaced peoples to fulfill God's global plan of redemption.

A REVEALED MYSTERY

Though the mystery of catastrophe is not some previously hidden prophecy that is now being discovered in the last days, it is a significant disclosure of revealed Bible truth in the last days. In this age of globalism and interconnected economies, it deeply affects how we view immigrants and refugees. It forces us to ask ourselves that if God is behind these global events, what should our spiritual and practical response be? Or if God is behind immigration and the displacing of people groups, then why are we so angry? If God is the initiator of global disasters and wars and they are not random and purposeless acts, we should try to understand why they might be happening rather than ignore or oppose them. Because God is the cause of the movements of people through catastrophe, he has a very clear standard for how foreigners are to be viewed and treated. In the Law, he tells the Hebrews: "if a resident alien lives with you in your land, you are not to mistreat him. You are to treat the resident alien the same way you treat the native born among you—love him like yourself, since you were foreigners in the land of Egypt" (Lev. 19:33-34, ISV). Jesus reiterated the same point: "And you shall love the Lord your God with all your heart and with all your soul and with all your mind and with all your strength.' The second is this: 'You shall love your neighbor as yourself.' There is no other commandment greater than these" (Mark 12:30-31, ESV).

When we elevate and promote our national or cultural interests in such a way that it leads to the mistreatment of the foreigner above the interests of God in the kind treatment of them, we have become sectarians and nationalists. I know this all too well, having lived in the Balkans for twenty-four years. There is even a word in the dictionary for this. It is called *Balkanization,* which means, "to divide a group or region into smaller regions or states that are often hostile to one another." In other words, hatred for the foreigner, or xenophobia. It is ugly and endless.

This is not a book about politics. In no way are we advocating open borders or lax immigration laws. Every responsible government should do all it can to protect its citizens from any foreign threats, and to enact and enforce fair yet strict immigration policies. The point I'm trying to make is that, as believers, when considering the issues of refugees and migrants, as in all matters, our first priority is to take our lead from Scripture not from political platforms. Our first priority must always be gospel centered.

If God brings disasters for the purpose of moving people from region to region and nation to nation so they may hear the message of salvation, and that his glory will fill the earth, then we can no longer simply look at foreigners, exiles, refugees and immigrants just from a political or national security perspective. God's purpose and plan is that they might be saved. He has given us instruction in how they are to be cared for, and He has given us the mandate to share the gospel with them. We have been given examples of how Jesus treated foreigners. Consider how He treated the Samaritan woman at the well. Though the Jews considered Samaritans as the worst of the human race because they were idolaters and considered half-breeds, Jesus was kind, spoke to the Samaritan woman and offered her living water. She was the lowly of the low for a Jew and yet Jesus offered her living water.

God has given us a big picture about the issue of foreigners. It is not a matter we can just dismiss as the result of bad political policies. God is the mover of the pieces on the chess board. "The king's heart is a stream of water in the hand of the LORD; he turns it wherever he will" (Pro. 21:1, ESV).

God's purposes will be fulfilled through bad rulers just as much as good ones. We should not forget that rulers are established by God for our good and for His glory. He raises them up and He puts them down. We may think we have the power to put people in positions of government, but the Scriptures make it clear it is God who makes these decisions (see Dan. 2:21). When these rulers do bad things, or make bad choices, it is by God's permission. He crafted the big picture, and He is causing events to occur which will ultimately lead to His desired end. Man's intention for doing evil will not trump God's plan for doing good. Just as God used Satan to bring about his desired end in the life of Job, so He uses the nations of the earth to bring about His purposes for the salvation of his world.

ISAIAH'S CALL

In Isaiah chapter 6 we see something startling and almost too difficult to believe. During Isaiah's encounter with God where he sees Him seated on His throne high and lifted up, the Lord said to him, "Whom shall I send, and who will go for us." Isaiah's reply: "Here I am! Send me." Then the Lord said this to him:

> Go and say to this people (Israel): "Keep on hearing but do not understand; keep on seeing but do not perceive. Make the heart of this people dull, and their ears heavy, and blind their eyes; lest they see with their eyes, and hear with their ears, and understand with their hearts, and turn and be healed." (Isaiah 6:9-10)

Did the Lord just commission Isaiah to go and preach to the people so that they will not understand or see or perceive? Did God just tell Isaiah to make the heart of the people dull, their eyes heavy and blind?! It appears so. This almost sounds too crazy to be true. Imagine God calling you to go to minister to a people for the purpose of preaching so that they will not listen to you because God does not want them to see or understand. Rather, He wants you to preach to them so that they become more hardened, more blinded, and more deaf!

Is this proof of the cruelty of God or the mercy of God? If we stop here one might be able to make a case for the former. Why in the world would God want His message to be preached only to have the hearts of the listeners further hardened than they already are? If we were to choose a central passage to prove the argument of this book, it would be right here. In this passage of Scripture, we discover the mystery of catastrophe. Here we find the nature of man, the nature of God, and the big picture of God's redemptive plan through catastrophe all rolled up into one.

In chapter 1 of Isaiah, God hands down His indictment to Israel. Because of Israel's continued sin and rebellion against God, they had become a people laden with iniquity. They had become so corrupted and so estranged from the Lord, they lost all perception of his holiness. Every part of Israel was sick, from the sole of the foot to the top of the head. God had already brought destruction, and they still would not repent. Israel was oblivious to its sinful ways and thought that by their external acts of worship and prayers they were okay before God, when in fact they were guilty, and their uplifted hands were full of blood.

Then beginning in verse sixteen, God gives to Israel eight steps they needed to take in repentance before He would forgive them and wash them from their sins:

1. Wash yourselves; make yourselves clean (v. 16)

2. Remove the evil of your deeds from before my eyes (v. 16)

3. Cease to do evil (v. 16)

4. Learn to do good (v. 17)

5. Seek justice (v. 17)

6. Correct oppression (v. 17)

7. Bring justice to the fatherless (v. 17)

8. Plead the widow's cause (v. 17)

These steps of repentance can be divided up into three parts:

Part 1: Taking personal responsibility for their actions (1-2)

Part 2: Deliberately learning to live differently (3-5)

Part 3: Proving their repentance by acts of justice and mercy (6-8)

It was only after taking these steps do we read,

Come now, let us reason together, says the Lord: though your sins are like scarlet, they shall be as white as snow; though they be red like crimson, they shall become like wool. (Isaiah 1:18)

This is so important for us in our understanding of true repentance. Repentance is when we turn away from our sin unto the Lord. It involves a volitional choice to

stop doing what is wrong before the eyes of the Lord,

learn to do what is right, and

live out works of righteousness to those in need of God's love and mercy.

At this point God told Israel that if they did these things, he would turn their blood-red sin into snow-white forgiveness. Then he gave this promise and warning: "If you are willing and obedient, you shall eat the good of the land; but if you refuse and rebel, you shall be eaten by the sword; for the mouth of the Lord has spoken" (Is. 1:19-20).

True repentance goes beyond just being willing to do what is right. There is a further step. It is called obedience. God said to Israel they must be willing *and* obedient. And if they were not both, they would be devoured by the sword.

Maybe there was a willingness on the part of Israel to live righteously, but there was no obedience. This strikes at the heart of man's nature. We may seem willing to do the right thing but fall short of it because our willingness never takes us far enough. It is like an alcoholic who is willing to give up alcohol when confronted about his drunkenness, but when temptation comes again he falls back into his old ways. Willingness never quite takes us to the 100 percent mark of repentance. But willingness coupled with obedience does.

This explains why God told Isaiah to preach a message that would lead to a further hardening of their hearts. Though Israel was already experiencing the destruction of their cities, and the desolation and overthrow of their land by foreigners, they were still hardened and unwilling to repent. Half-hearted repentance is no repentance at all. Israel had not suffered enough loss to break them and cause them to turn to the Lord with their entire heart. They had to be afflicted significantly more before they would call out to God in true and full repentance. Isaiah asks the Lord how long he was to preach this message. Then the Lord said:

> Until cities lie waste without inhabitant, and houses without people, and the land is a desolate waste, and the LORD removes people far away, and the forsaken places are many in the midst of the land. And though a tenth remain in it, it will be burned again, like a terebinth or an oak, whose stump remains when it is felled. The holy seed is its stump. (Isaiah 6:11-13)

The Lord called Isaiah to proclaim a message to make the heart of the people dull, to further blind their eyes, and to give them even less perception and understanding in order to cause further destruction, misery, and hardship so that Israel would not partially repent but fully repent. Because the whole body was sick, the whole body needed to be healed. If only fifty percent of cancer is removed from the body, the cancer is still there. To bring complete healing, the cancer has to be removed entirely. God is not interested in half-hearted surrender. He pursues man that He may gain his whole heart and soul. He wants this for Israel, His church and for all nations.

Here again we see God's use of catastrophe to accomplish His divine purpose of salvation. Salvation is the theme of Isaiah. He had to lay waste the cities until there were no inhabitants, destroy the land and scatter people as refugees into foreign lands. He destroyed that he might build. He laid waste the he might renew. He scattered that he might gather. He blinded that he might give sight. He wounded that he might heal. Only a very good God would go to these lengths to save a people.

PAUL ON MARS HILL

The most remarkable passage in all the Bible referring to God's goal of salvation of all nations by way of migration is found in Acts:

And he made from one man every nation of mankind to live on all the face of the earth, having determined allotted periods and the boundaries of their dwelling place, that they should seek God, and perhaps feel their way toward him and find him. Yet he is actually not far from each one of us. (Acts 17:26-27)

Paul, in his message to the Athenians on Mars Hill, gave to the unregenerate gentiles the purpose and plan of God for them and the world. It is that man may be fruitful and multiply and fill the earth so that he may seek after God in salvation and find Him. Paul further declared that it is God who determines their times—*when they live*—and their places of habitation—*where they live.*

When we see wars and natural disasters, which lead to refugee crises and mass migration, we should think about this passage. It is clear that God's purpose is to move people across the face of the globe so that his salvation and glory might spread to the very ends of the earth.

The Greeks themselves quite possibly migrated from the north as Indo-Europeans to Greece.[1] It was at the Areopagus, near the Acropolis where Paul preached this message. The Acropolis is where the first Athenians settled thousands of years before. Did Paul know that? I'm certain he did. Standing near the very rock of their origins, he proclaimed that it was God who brought them there, and it was in that very same spot where he proclaimed to them the Good News of Jesus Christ!

God allotted their times so they would be there in that moment of history, and He determined that location to be their appointed place of habitation that they may hear the message of salvation, seek God, and perhaps find Him. O, the wonder and mystery of God! How vast is His wisdom and great is His love for mankind!

Several years ago, I (Nathan) was walking in the area of the Acropolis. I was there with my wife and children. I was intent on finding the monument to the unknown god Paul referred to: "For as I passed along and observed the objects of your worship, I found also an altar with this inscription: 'To the unknown god.' What therefore you worship as unknown, this I proclaim to you" (Acts 17:23).

It seemed like hours of looking at all the altars and monuments before I finally found it. There obscurely lying on the ground, surrounded by clumps of withering grass was a very small slab of stone. Obviously etched in English for the tourists to read were the words "To the unknown god." Excitedly, I called my family over to see. I still have the picture standing with my two sons next to the spot.

Paul's interest of Athens must have been acute and his powers of observation keen to have taken notice of such an obscure altar. As God allotted the times of the Athenians to hear Paul's message, He allotted Paul's time to be there to see that slab of stone, and to use those words to launch his powerful message to the Greeks. Paul informed them that their unknown god is the God who made the world and all things in it, the Lord of heaven and earth. He is the God who gives life and breath to all mankind and to every living thing. From Him came all the nations of the earth that they may seek after and find Him. And this God, Paul proclaimed to them, is not unknown at all, but is a God who is ever present and near to all who call upon him.

Matthew Soerens is the US Director of Church Mobilization at World Relief. Daniel Darling is an author, speaker, and columnist. They wrote an article that touches on this passage and immigration. They say, "While economic and sociological reasons drive people's desire to migrate, we believe God has sovereignly superintended this movement of people to America so that they might come into a saving relationship with Jesus Christ and follow him as disciples."[2]

It is primarily through catastrophe that He determines the times and places of the nations and peoples of the earth. God uses natural and man-made disasters as His primary means of driving people to geographic locations of His choosing for the times of His choosing, to specifically position them to hear and believe in the one and only true God and salvation through His Son, Jesus Christ.

THE GLOBAL MIGRATION OF PEOPLE

From what we see in the Bible, all families from all nations can trace their origins back to Adam and Eve in the garden of Eden. The story of America is the story of migration, and the origins of this nation can be attributed to the pilgrims who fled Europe to escape religious persecution. Supposedly, even the American Indian migrated from Asia across the Bearing Strait. The story of Europeans, Asians, Africans, Australians, and the rest of the populated continents can trace their histories back to some other place.

Humans have been migrating since the dawn of time. We have always been in motion, relentless in our drive across the face of the earth. This movement of people will continue until the saints of Jesus Christ proclaim the gospel to all nations, and the peoples of the earth one day are filled with the knowledge of God. This is God's plan, His purpose, and His will. Migration in its many forms will not cease until God's glory fills the earth and all ethnic groups are exposed to the gospel message, and at least some from each are safely brought into the kingdom of God. This movement of people is actually the movement of God for His world.

There are a record 65 million refugees in the world today, more than at any other time since records have been taken. This is approximately 1 out of every 113 people in the world! In 2015 some twenty-four people were displaced from their homes every minute of every day. Almost half of them were from the Muslim world.[3] They are all part of God's program. In this program, it is the privilege and responsibility of the church to respond to both their physical and spiritual needs. Christians should be the first in line to meet them and greet them in the name of Jesus.

Regardless of what our governments do, it should be the undisputed policy of the global church of Jesus Christ to extend the love of God to refugees in foreign lands, and when they arrive in our own.

If God were anywhere near completing His strategy of distributing and redistributing people around the globe through disasters, we would see some kind of slowing but we don't. Instead the pace has only increased, and it has increased exponentially. Alarm bells should be going off. The increased activity should tell us that God is up to something and we need to be ready to respond strategically and quickly with tremendous amounts of human and financial resources. Doors are opening wide for the proclamation of the gospel to many people who have lived their entire lives in spiritual darkness but may finally be given opportunity to enter into the light.

I once heard someone say, "Displaced people are not misplaced by God." What powerful and insightful words. Our places of habitation determined by God may or may not be the place of our origin. In fact, you may trace your ancestry back only a few generations to somewhere in Europe or elsewhere. Just because someone was born in one country does not mean that will be their permanent residence or the country of their descendants. God may have another plan for them to dwell somewhere else as He did for Abraham, and for millions of exiles fleeing war and other disasters over the centuries.

These precious souls caught in an upside-down and chaotic world are not misplaced. Albeit many are living in extreme conditions, in kindness and gentle mercy, God is carefully placing them nonetheless. His desire is for them to come out of darkness and into His marvelous light. Catastrophe is darkness, but it is from this darkness that God brings them to the light.

"It has been difficult for me and my family to be here. It isn't easy to look at suffering day in and day out. I can't imagine experiencing the kinds of suffering I am seeing around me. I hug my children a little bit tighter and longer each night before they go to bed. I watch out for my wife more than I ever have in the past. The reality of the brutality of man is ever present. I only read about the kinds of unspeakable raping of a people, but never before was witness to it. It makes one realize more fully what we ought to truly value in life."

—KOSOVAR REFUGEE CRISIS, PERSONAL JOURNAL, MAY 7, 1999

PRESENT-DAY EXAMPLES

He reveals mysteries from the darkness and brings the deep darkness into light.
—JOB 12:22

BEFORE THE LARGEST REFUGEE CRISIS since WWII was unleashed in Europe in 2015, God had already set the stage. Beginning in the late 1980s and early 1990s, the atheistic empire of communism collapsed in Eastern Europe and the Balkans. When this colossal domino fell it paved the way for the rapid expansion of Christianity and subsequently prepared the church to respond to two of the largest refugee crises of our times in Kosovo and Syria.

THE KOSOVO CONFLICT

When I was crying next to the sixteen-year-old boy and asking God why he had to suffer so much, little did I know the plan of God for his nation of Kosovo. When my family and I arrived to begin our work in Albania in January 1994, we came as pioneers to an unreached country. For nearly fifty years, Albania suffered under one of the most brutal communist systems in the world. I often tell people if they want to know what it was like during those years, look at North Korea today. There really are no words to describe the conditions of that time. It was beyond deplorable.

In 1967 the communist leader Enver Hoxha declared Albania to be the first officially atheistic nation in the world.[1] Hoxha, more than all communist leaders, wanted to establish a pure Stalinist system. In 1972, he severed relations with China because he felt they had become imperialistic like the United States.[2] Albania was known as the most hermit country in the world. The leaders looked inward, closing the country's doors to most other nations and turned it into the most repressive and poorest country in Europe. The religion of Albania was Albanianism. God was ruthlessly thrown out, and most vestiges of religion were completely shattered. One could not even mention the name God for fear of imprisonment or death. More than a third of the population worked as informants for the government, making the people paranoid and living in absolute fear.

When communism fell in the spring of 1991, many Albanians fled to escape the dreadful conditions and lack of opportunity. It was at that time missionaries began flooding the nation, spreading the message of salvation throughout the country. Within a short period of time, the church was reborn, and many Albanians came to faith in Christ. The people who were once prevented from knowing anything about God were starving spiritually, and it didn't take long before several thousand had placed their faith in Jesus. An amazing movement of God was happening in the once closed, atheistic land of Albania.

Just across the northern border from Albania was Serbia, another formerly communist nation. Within its borders was Kosovo, a region populated with more than 90 percent Muslims, who were ethnic Albanians. Kosovo was a difficult place for the gospel. Until 1999 there were between only four to six very small evangelical churches in the country, each averaging no more than eight to ten people. But God had a plan for the salvation of Kosovo through catastrophe. It is a reality my family and I have had the privilege and difficulty of observing and participating in.

Many years ago, when I was just a sophomore in high school sitting in my sociology class flipping through a geography book, I came to the section on Albania. There was a picture of an Albanian farmer sitting on a hay wagon. Below the picture was a caption that said something to the effect that this man is from the most isolated, Stalinist, and atheistic country in the world.

It was 1979, and I had been saved for only a couple of years. I had no idea what missions was, or even Christian service for that matter. I only knew that God saved me, and all I wanted to do was tell other people about Him. But as I looked down at the man on the wagon, God spoke to my heart and burned the image into my mind. To this day, when I think of him, I can still make out the details of the man's face. It was one of those lightning bolt moments that one experiences only rarely in life. At that moment, the Lord spoke into my heart and said, *"I want you to go to this man's country to preach the gospel."* It was an undeniably incredible experience that to this day I cannot explain. The experience was so powerful that I still find myself looking for the man on the hay wagon.

In 1979 communism was raging and threatening to spread throughout the world. With the little information I had, I began researching Albania and soon discovered that it would be impossible for me to go for two reasons: I was an American and I was a Christian. But the encounter that day in my sociology class was so profound, I knew God wanted me to go, and from that point on I made it my life's goal to one day carry the gospel to Albania.

Since that time, I have heard stories similar to mine of God calling people to former communist countries. The reason? God knew what He was about to do in Eastern Europe. He was about to demolish the Iron Curtain of communism that shrouded people in lies and denied them the opportunity to know about Him. In the sovereign strategy of God, He was taking preemptive measures by preparing a new generation to be missionaries to freshly opened countries. My wife and I were privileged to be among them.

In Albania, where not even an underground church existed, God raised up the body of Christ before dealing with Kosovo. From 1991 until 1999 the Albanian church grew exponentially. Then in 1999 Serbian leader Slobodan Milosevic began his brutal campaign to ethnically cleanse Kosovo of Albanians, leading to a war and a massive refugee crisis. That same year God, through the catastrophic war, brought the nation of Kosovo to Albania in the form of hundreds of thousands of refugees.

When they arrived, it was the evangelical Christians in Albania who were among the first on the scene to receive them. They were the young Christians who came to faith in Christ over the previous eight years. They received the Kosovar refugees into their homes, churches, and camps managed by Christians. Refugees were given food, clothing, housing, medical care and supplies, jobs . . . and the gospel. As a result, many Kosovar exiles came to faith in Christ. When they returned home after the war, many expatriate missionaries and Albanian nationals followed them back.

As the result of a major regional catastrophe, God drove these refugees from Kosovo to Albania and into the arms of His beloved body. As a result of the Albanian churches recognizing this opportunity, responding quickly, and doing what they were supposed to do, today in the Muslim country of Kosovo, the church has grown from four very small churches before 1999 to more than forty today, with hundreds of believers.

God brought catastrophe to Kosovo, but He timed it perfectly. Twenty years before, He spoke to the heart of a young fifteen-year-old boy, along with a whole generation of other young men and women. He put a burden on our hearts for the communist world. He led us to pray and to prepare ourselves for this future service. While He was doing this, He was orchestrating geopolitical events that led to the ripping down of the Iron Curtain. When the curtain fell, He sent His workers to storm the cities and countryside with the gospel. Before fully opening Kosovo, He first readied His church in Albania to respond to the disaster He then brought to Kosovo later.

God tore Kosovo to pieces that His life might spring forth in the hearts of wounded, devastated, and disillusioned Muslim refugees. He drove them out as exiles of war that He might save them. But what is most significant to capture here is that God prepared His church before He brought catastrophe—first in Albania, then in Kosovo. We cannot miss this vital tactic of God. *Before God unleashes calamities, He always raises up, prepares, and positions His people to respond with compassion and words of eternal life when disasters strike.*

SYRIAN REFUGEE CRISIS

This amazing story of Albania and Kosovo does not end here. In this divine strategy of God, He brought catastrophe to Albania, Kosovo, and other Balkan nations so they would then be prepared to participate in an even larger catastrophe to come: the Syrian refugee crisis.

In what began as part of the Arab Spring, anti-government demonstrations in Syria started in March 2011. In a country of 23 million people, almost half of the population have either fled the country or are internally displaced, due to civil war.[3] Besides the number of people who have been injured or who have fled the war, over 470,000 have been killed.[4] Today the Syrian crisis has become the biggest humanitarian disaster of our times, with Syrians representing the largest refugee population in the world.[5]

By 2015, more than 2 million refugees spilled over into Turkey. In that same year, thousands were arriving into the southeastern Balkans. By September, as many as five thousand refugees a day were making their way up from Greece into Macedonia, Serbia, Croatia, and into other parts of Europe.[6] In 2015 More than a million migrants and refugees traveled from the Middle East into Europe, making it what the *Irish Times* called, "a year expected to exceed all previous records for global forced displacement."[7]

In fall 2014, before the dam broke, and the flood of refugees began streaming across the Balkans into Western Europe, Joel Richardson and I held a major regional conference with more than two hundred pastors and leaders from eleven nations in and around the region. The focus of the conference was to discuss worst-case scenarios and the role Christian leaders and their churches should take in the event of major geopolitical changes, or the rise of radical Islam in the region.

At the conferences were workshops in which we proposed initiatives for how these young, first generation leaders should respond in the event another major catastrophe should strike the Balkans, which are the geographic gateway between the Middle East and Europe. Little did any of us know just how timely this conference would be. Within months of the event, a massive influx of humanity, tens of thousands of refugees and migrants from the Middle East and Central Asia transited week after week through the Balkan corridor into Western Europe.

Then, as they had in previous disasters, many of the pastors and leaders who attended the conference in 2014 organized to respond to this new catastrophe. Moving quickly to border transit points the Christians met the transiting refugees and migrants, nationals and expatriate workers from Greece, Hungary, Macedonia, Croatia, Serbia, Bosnia, Kosovo and Albania and mobilized humanitarian aid and shared the gospel to the predominantly Muslim exiles.

The migrants and refugees would arrive from Turkey into Greece by small rafts before being processed and transported north by train or bus. In most cases, once they arrived at the transit points, their stay was generally short, often no more than several minutes before walking to the next bordering country. The nature of the crisis gave little to no time to get to know or talk to the people. In order to spend any time at all with the refugees, they had to walk with them for two to three kilometers between borders to hear their stories and pray for them.

Due to the massive numbers and their constantly being on the move, it was impossible to reach most of the refugees, but many of them were reached. News from various locations was encouraging with as many as five to seven Muslims coming to faith in Christ daily at one border point alone. Believers distributed tens of thousands of micro SD cards for smart phones that were loaded with Scripture and other Christian resources.

Believers would discover gaps that formed between borders and camps along the refugee routes to walk with them to assist in any way they could. It was an awesome site to see Albanians from Kosovo interacting with those in the camps. Their connection was immediate. It began with words like these, "I was once a Muslim and war refugee who had to flee my country just like you. While I was an exile in a foreign country, I heard about Jesus Christ. I would like to tell you about Him."

Though the response from national Christians and expatriate workers made a difference, there were only a handful of people to reach the thousands we encountered daily. It was barely enough. The sea of people was too much to manage on their own. While Christians in the West debated the political and security implications of refugees coming from Syria, a small band of brave and faithful servants stood on the front lines day after day to meet the exiles as they moved along the narrow passage through their tiny countries.

An opportunity of an unprecedented scale was handed to the church. In extraordinary numbers God guided the nations of the Middle East by the hundreds of thousands directly into the path of His church. Few recognized the opportunity and fewer faithfully and tirelessly responded, but the vast majority of the behemoth church of Jesus Christ did not. It could have been one of the greatest harvests of Muslims to Christ ever, but that has not happened yet. There are still great things happening as Christians in Germany, Austria, Holland and other western European countries have received many of these refugees, who are coming to faith in Christ. Praise God for the many who did hear and believe, but the optimum moment has passed. The great Muslim migration of 2015 has come and gone.

But this is not the end of the story, and this is most certainly not the last opportunity we will have. These kinds of mass refugee and migrant crises will happen with more frequency. God is unveiling this mystery of catastrophe to help us prepare for what awaits us and them. As we learn more about this, we also need to be on guard against the schemes of the devil. In the same way that God has a strategy to save the world through catastrophe, Satan has a plan to destroy the world through the same. Part of that strategy is to divide and distract Christians from these movements of God long enough to keep them from responding in time or even at all.

TRACKING GOD'S MOVEMENTS

These and other refugee crises are serving as present-day examples of what the church of Jesus Christ can and must do in the future. With this better understanding of God's purpose in catastrophe, and how it serves as His primary apparatus for scattering people in order to draw large numbers of the lost to Himself, we can be better prepared to respond. Also, examining what led to the timing of these two catastrophes, we have been able to track to some degree the strategic movements of God, going all the way back prior to the fall of communism. The following is what we have observed:

- Like with Abraham, God's first step is to call out a generation of men and women to prepare themselves for something He would later show them.

- Those who step out to be prepared for future service, understand that one day others will be blessed with the hope of salvation by their act of faith.

- While His people are being prepared, God aligns the political and geographic chess pieces for these great, catastrophic events.

- At the designated time, catastrophes strike and people are scattered.

- Simultaneously, those He called and prepared for the moment are positioned and mobilized to respond for a great harvest of souls.

- As a result of catastrophe and the mobilization of Christ's witnesses, many are saved.

Kosovo and Syria are only two examples of this occurring. Other stories can be told where this similar pattern has unfolded since the collapse of communism. This is not random. It appears to be designed by God for the last days.

If this is a consistent strategy God uses, then it is not unreasonable for us to conclude that God wants us to see what is coming and how we should prepare. In the same way that we have tracked the movements of God as it relates to Kosovo and Syria, what if we could reasonably forecast the same for where these catastrophes may happen in the future? What if by tracking the past movements of God in catastrophe, we can reasonably forecast His next big moves? Could it be that this is exactly what God wants us to do?

In the end times, we are being given an opportunity to peer into a magnificent mystery of God. The big picture of God's global movements of people through disaster is being unveiled, and we are supremely privileged to be a part of it.

"Today my family and I got up from bed and decided it would be a day of rejoicing. In such dark times, as the NATO planes continued flying overhead, we needed to be reminded that God is on His throne and that Jesus is alive. Lorraine was in the kitchen reading the account of Christ's crucifixion. As she was contemplating the significance of His sacrifice, my son Justin (five) came in to the kitchen and asked her why she was crying. She said, "I just read about Jesus dying on the cross, and it made me sad." Justin looked at her and said, "Mommy, don't cry. Look at the next page. He's alive."

—KOSOVAR REFUGEE CRISIS, PERSONAL JOURNAL, APRIL 4, 1999 (EASTER SUNDAY)

THE BIG PICTURE OF CATASTROPHE

I know that you can do all things, and that no purpose of yours can be thwarted.

—JOB 42:2

THE INSPIRATION FOR ACHIEVING great things comes from being challenged to do the impossible. The esteemed missionary William Carey once said, "Expect great things from God; attempt great things for God." When God speaks to us to follow Him in his global movements, He generally casts the big picture before moving to the details. He begins with the larger vision and then moves to the particulars: *"For God so loved the world . . ."* (big picture) *"that whosoever"* (the particular).

When we endeavor to inspire others by casting a small vision and then move to a larger mission from there, we limit our capacity and the capacity of others to expect great things from God, or attempt great things for Him. What is more inspiring for a coach to tell his team: "Guys, let's try and win our first game, then the next and the next, and, if we do that, we might make it to the regionals." Or for the coach to say: "Guys, I really believe we can win State this year. We are going to work and discipline ourselves to be the best. I believe we can do it, and it begins by winning our first game." The first is a blasé pep talk at best, uninspiring and lacking altogether in vision. The second is an inspiring challenge to high achievement. The first talk begins with the small and moves to the larger. The second begins with the grand and moves to the first win.

For many, this idea of God wanting us to engage global disasters may seem too daunting and intimidating. In times like these, we need to remember who we are. We are the church of the living God. There is no greater power and no stronger authority on earth than the power of God working through His body. The influence of the church of Jesus Christ in this world is enormous, so great that even the powers of darkness cannot prevail against it.

God is casting the big picture for us to see because He made us to face the global sized challenges He brings our way. We may feel like we can only do small things, but God made us for big things. We tend to be too provincial in how we view ourselves and our role in this world, but God wants us to see how much He loves the entire world. He wants us to see the vital part we play in His plan to save it, so that He might share the inheritance of the nations with us one day. The church is God's spiritual institution through which He is working triumphantly on this earth. And if this is true, we have to understand and boldly accept the God-sized tasks we have been given.

Never in the history of the church has there been greater opportunity and greater ability to fully engage each catastrophe God brings. So, when we move with God, we are moving in unison and partnership with Him to be His ready instruments to bind up wounds, feed the hungry, clothe the naked and bring good news to those affected and fleeing when disaster strikes.

This is not something we can outsource to others. The United Nations, secular NGOs, and government agencies might do a good job at providing and coordinating relief, but they are also the very ones who oppose the gospel. They are the ones who are generally blocking Christians from fulfilling their foremost responsibility of preaching the Good News to those affected by crisis. So long as Christian churches and organizations stick to giving aid and assisting in other humanitarian projects, they are tolerated, and, even, sometimes given important responsibilities from those groups, so long as they do not "proselytize." It is our privilege and duty to provide humanitarian aid to those in need, but that is not our mandate. Our mandate is to make disciples of all nations.

When the church fails to show up when catastrophes strike, the consequences are profound. The enemies of God are always crouching at the door, looking for every opportunity to swoop in and seize the day. When the church does not show up, others will, but God did not commission the United Nations High Commission for Refugees (UNHCR) to do our job. He did not raise up the Islamic Relief Organization to substitute for us. God did not call the Red Cross to be His hands and feet to those impacted by natural and man-made disasters. He commissioned and raised up and called us—the church of the living God to powerfully and triumphantly lead the way. When it comes to people's souls, we need not cower to any human institution, regardless of the powers they hold. Their mandate is the Geneva Convention; ours is the clarion call to preach the gospel to all nations.

FINISHING THE GREAT COMMISSION

The central theme of all the Bible, the thread that runs through the whole of Scripture is the filling of the whole earth with the glory of God in the salvation of the nations. What God commissioned Israel to do is the same as what Jesus commissioned His disciples to do. The mandate was passed from Israel to the church and it will continue until the task is completed.

For Israel God said, "It is too light a thing that you should be my servant to raise up the tribes of Jacob and to bring back the preserved of Israel; I will make you as a light for the nations, that my salvation may reach to the end of the earth." (Is. 49:6, ESV).

For the church God said, "Go therefore and make disciples of all nations, baptizing them in the name of the Father and of the Son and of the Holy Spirit, teaching them to observe all that I have commanded you. And behold I am with you always, to the end of the age" (Matt. 28:19-20, ESV).

When God gave this command, He intended for it to be accomplished. It has never been the plan of God for this command, to disciple all nations, to fall short in any measure. It was a call, not for a partial win, but for total victory. God will not stop His pursuit of man until He has gained every last kindred and tongue and people and nation on earth. Obviously not every person will be saved, but it is God's divine plan to claim some from all *ethne* (people group). The death of Christ was not in vain. The Father will gain what He sent His Son to win, but He has commissioned the Christians to bring them in.

So, when the church fails to understand the big picture, when it misses God's larger redemptive purposes in the mass movements of people through catastrophe, it misses some of the greatest opportunities. These are the special moments that the Lord has given us to help complete the job of gospel proclamation. Jesus said, "My Father is always at his work to this very day, and I too am working" (John 5:17, NIV). God is constantly moving, and we must move with Him. God is continually strategizing for the nations, and we must strategize with Him.

If believers resist the global movements of people as migrants, exiles, and refugees due to their political views, and nationalistic, or ethnic sensibilities, it is very likely they are resisting a great work of God in a massive movement of unreached peoples to Christ. When the church resists and puts up barriers to these people, it very well may be resisting a divine undertaking of God and preventing them from hearing the gospel, thus hindering the Great Commission from being fulfilled.

When we fail to see what God is doing in the displacement of people through catastrophe, it has eternal consequences for the very ones God wants to save. If these wandering exiles do not hear, they will die in their sins and never experience peace with God through Jesus Christ. We are the very ones He is driving them to. When we hinder their movements to where they can hear the good news, we cause an even greater tragedy for them than the crises from which they are fleeing.

THE STRATEGY OF GOD

I (Nathan) learned the value of strategy when I played Indiana high school basketball. In those days, there were no class divisions of high schools. If you were a school of two hundred or two thousand, it didn't matter. Regardless of the size, all teams would strive to win the one and only prestigious title of Indiana State Basketball Champion. Remember the movie *Hoosiers*? To reach any level of state-wide success, the smaller your school was, the more strategic it had to be. If a coach couldn't win by height, talent, and speed, he had to find other ways to win games. That could happen only by good discipline and excellent strategies.

A strategy is "a plan, method, or series of maneuvers or stratagems for obtaining a specific goal or result."[1] God is the ultimate strategist. Throughout history, He has been moving people and nations to fulfill an end goal—that His glory will fill the whole earth, in the salvation of all nations. And God is obtaining this goal by implementing plans, methods and a series of maneuvers and stratagems in the world for it to be accomplished through us. It is through this lens that we better understand what Paul meant when he wrote: "But God chose the foolish things of the world to shame the wise; God chose the weak things of the world to shame the strong" (1 Cor. 1:27, NIV).

The most strategic plan does not always involve using the biggest, best, and most obvious solution. Sometimes it is about utilizing whatever resources are available in the most creative and disciplined manner possible to fulfill your ultimate objectives. When planning for a battle, an army doesn't necessarily plan for a direct assault. It looks at the whole picture and examines the weaknesses of the enemy to determine the most strategic place to attack. It may mean using smaller forces coming from unsuspecting locations to take out key positions. Sometimes what is popular or obvious may be the least effective in the long run.

In constantly trying to tap into God's strategies for the nations, we don't believe God is necessarily interested in the big and popular trends we often attach ourselves to and try and replicate. Those trends can be distractions to what is actually planned by God. If our mandate is to make disciples of ALL nations, then how does God want to use us to do that, with the limited people and resources we have? If we follow what is popular we may find personal fulfillment in pursuing what many others are doing, but does it do anything to fulfill the ALL of the Great Commission?

Catastrophe has been God's primary apparatus for achieving His grand strategy for all nations from the beginning of time. It is a major part of God's blueprint to draw all nations to Himself. In the same manner that a good coach follows his proven strategies and tactics to win games, God does the same to win souls. This sovereign strategy of God has been implemented and proven since the dawn of mankind, and it is not about to change.

It is shortsighted to see catastrophes only as judgments from God. It is clear throughout the Bible that God has brought disaster for the purpose of judgment, but that is only as a last resort. James declares that "mercy triumphs over judgment" (James 2:13). In his deliberate and constant pursuit of man, God seeks after lost sinners to bring them in to His fold. His plans are to use things that confound us to find those who will come to Him and lay their lives down at the foot of the cross in submission to Jesus Christ. The One who loved them to the point of death will go to the farthest corners of the earth to find them: "For the Son of Man came to seek and save the lost" (Luke 19:10, ESV). In this big picture, God drives out the lost as migrants, exiles, and refugees by way of the crucible of catastrophe and human suffering. Where He drives them is directly into the waiting arms of His people. And when His people are scattered due to natural and man-made disasters, they are sent to "all nations" in order to fulfill His redemptive plan for the world.

Since God is the divine strategist it is essential that we discover what those strategies are and then move to develop our own stratagems that line up with His. If catastrophe is central to His plan for the nations, then it is imperative that we reassess how we are attempting to reach the nations in the last days. God is trying to show us something from the past, the present, and what will happen in the future. If mission minded churches and mission agencies want to be the vanguards of the most advanced movements of God in the world, they need to adapt their approaches to the paradigm of global catastrophes. History, and, especially, the present clearly reveal this.

God's word makes it crystal clear that what we are seeing today is only a drop in the bucket compared to what is coming. If we are not preemptive and do not track or forecast well the movements of God in the scattering of the nations and then proactively move to position ourselves for these eventualities, we will be left standing in the dust. In light of this, if we decide to stick to our lumbering policies that dictate a "wait and see" approach, we will be left scratching our heads wondering what just happened. When catastrophes strike, we will still be sitting in conference rooms trying to decide what to do long after the crisis has past and the opportunities are gone. If we do, we will be ensuring our own failure to move when God moves. We cannot allow that to happen.

The mission of God is too important for us to not be strategic in these times. The present haphazard, shotgun approach we often take to the mandate to make disciples of all nations does not serve the church of Jesus Christ, nor the world, well. It is eternally more important to track the movements of God and adapt our methods to those movements than it is to track the popular generational or missional trends that are more often based on cultural, pragmatic, or politically correct considerations.

ALL NATIONS STRATEGY

Haiti is a nation of ten million people. According to Operation World about 95 percent of the country claims to be Christian.[2] It is one of the most evangelized countries of the world. Not only has Haiti been evangelized, it has been evangelized over and over and over again. Haiti is awash with Christian evangelism and humanitarian aid. It is a country overly saturated by churches and Christian organizations, and more keep going.

Before the 2010 earthquake in Haiti, there were approximately seventeen hundred career missionaries in the country. Thousands more short-term teams go to train pastors and leaders and plant churches. Since 1804, Haiti has been a popular destination for missionaries.[3] That is more than two hundred years of missionary work in this tiny Caribbean island. How much more do we think Haiti needs before it takes on the responsibility to lead itself? How many Haitians have been sent from Haiti as missionaries? Not very many. When a nation like Haiti is always the receiving country, there is not much incentive for the national believers to be contributors. It is just too easy to keep receiving.

The amounts of money, aid, and resources poured into this tiny nation over the years must be staggering, possibly in the billions of dollars. Google "Haiti missions" and see for yourself. Count how many times you will see mission to Haiti, then count how many times you read missions from Haiti. Yet there are entire people groups in the world, many of them ten times the population of Haiti that have never been reached with the gospel. How do we answer for this? Is God calling everyone to Haiti and none to these peoples? When Jesus commissioned His disciples, He told them to go into all nations, not some nations. We have been very effective in employing a "some nations" strategy, which is man's strategy, and have missed the mark considerably in an "all nations" strategy, which is God's strategy.

Is Haiti a poor nation that has great need? Certainly. No one would dispute that. But what about the rest of the world? According to the Joshua Project, 40 percent of the people groups of the world are still unreached with the gospel.[4] Most of them live in what is called the 10/40 Window. This is a rectangular region of North Africa, the Middle East, and Asia located between ten and forty degrees north latitude.[5] This is where two-thirds of the world's population resides and where most of the unreached peoples on earth are. It is also where 85 percent of the world's poorest dwell.[6]

Our purpose here is not to denigrate or lessen the value of those who have given their lives to serve the people of Haiti. It is also not to put into question their sincere, godly efforts and desire to reach Haitians. Our purpose is to raise an awareness of what God wants to do globally, and hopefully to challenge the church to see the larger picture of what God is telling us to do in light of catastrophe and the end times. It is imperative that we understand what this means and take seriously the importance of employing good, wise, and sound strategies for reaching all nations with the gospel. By the power of God and the leading of His Spirit, the task is achievable, but we must be prayerful and smart about what we do as we enter into an ever-increasingly complicated and dangerous world.

FROM EVERYWHERE TO EVERYWHERE

William Carey, the father of modern missions, began a missionary undertaking from England to India and set in motion, for the next 250 years, a movement from Western Europe and America to the rest of the world. Over the next two centuries, Christianity spread globally into the remotest parts of the earth. As Christianity has grown in parts of the world such as South America, East and Southeast Asia, and Eastern Europe, the church in those areas has begun responding to do its part in fulfilling the Great Commission. Over this past generation an amazing movement of God has been taking place. The global mission movement has shifted from being unidirectional to multidirectional. It is often called the global south movement or the majority world movement.

Though Western Europe and America still play a very strong and leading role in training and sending missionaries, the paradigm is no longer from the West to the rest, but from everywhere to everywhere. God is raising up His church globally from some of the most unlikely places on earth to send His laborers into the harvest fields to reach those who have never heard.

This explains an important tactic of God in the last days. He is calling out His body from multiple points around the world in order to position His church to respond to the exponential rise of global catastrophes. He is giving believers from all nations the opportunity to participate in bringing in the remaining harvest, many of whom will come into the kingdom as a result of natural and man-made disasters.

God is not only shifting and repositioning the nations of the world to hear about Him, He is also shifting and repositioning His church to meet the growing challenges of reaching those who are being and will be impacted by the disasters brought by Him. The big question is, do we see it? Are we recognizing what God is doing, or are we simply going on our merry way, seeing these changes as only glitches and anomalies to our business as usual? If we do, then we do it at the peril of souls and the loss of what could be our greatest moment in history.

MOVING WHEN GOD MOVES

We may also be missing an unprecedented movement of God among the nations in the last days. God is not provincial. His goal is global. His desire is that the whole body of Christ, not just some, participate in the harvesting of the nations. From the rapidly changing geopolitics, the exponential rise of global disasters—and the movement of large groups of people due to those disasters—to the global expansion of the church, we can see that God is on the verge of something great, the likes of which we have never seen before.

The church's new mission statement should read, Moving When God Moves. We can have no better rallying cry than this. The pace at which everything is racing ahead globally, whether it be with information, technology, communications, or transportation, has accelerated beyond anything seen before. According to *Industry Tap* magazine, until 1900, human knowledge doubled approximately every century. By WWII it was doubling every twenty-five years. Today, knowledge doubles every thirteen months, but that is soon to increase to every twelve hours![7]

The article goes on to say,

> In a recent lecture at Harvard University neuroscientist Jeff Lichtman, who is attempting to map the human brain, has calculated that several billion petabytes of data storage would be needed to index

the entire human brain. The Internet is currently estimated to be 5 million terabytes (TB) of which Google has indexed roughly 200 TB or just .004% of its total size. The numbers involved are astounding especially when considering the size of the human brain and the number of neurons in it. . . . A transition from the linear growth of the human knowledge to the exponential growth of the human brain has taken place.[8]

While the global movers and shakers in industry, technology and communications are adapting, and even setting the pace for these global changes, the church's strategies, movements, and methods for keeping up with these changes to reach the remaining 40 percent of the world's unreached population are not. Though many are making modifications, on the most part we are not keeping up—not even close. Although the world is speeding by—no longer at the speed of light, but at quantum speed—the church is lumbering along at a snail's pace. While the message we preach remains the same, the strategies for effectively reaching people need to keep pace with technology. Sadly, much of what we see today is the reverse. Rather than churches and mission organizations modifying their methods for delivering their pure and uncompromising message of the gospel, many are compromising the message and maintaining the same, antiquated systems.

With the jump from linear growth of knowledge to exponential growth, it is as though everything is moving faster these days. And when we look at the increase in catastrophes it is as though God is hurrying up His plans. The sharp increase of migration, geopolitical changes, and disasters happening in the world indicate a faster pace for the movements of God, but the church and missions are not keeping up.

In God's narrative, the plot is gaining tension and momentum for the story's climax. God is setting the stage for His grand end times events that will usher in the King of kings and Lord of lords. God is showing us the big picture. This is our wake-up call to respond wisely, prayerfully, urgently, and strategically to gather in the nations.

Part 2

WHAT COMES NEXT?
(Joel Richardson)

"Why did you leave?" At this question, the father turned silent, turned away from the camera and began to cry. In a common Muslim expression of compassion, I put my hand over my heart and said, "I'm sorry. I'm sorry." He turned back to me with tears streaming down his face and began telling us of the war in Syria, all the explosions around their house and how they had lost everything. They, like thousands of others had fled for their lives. When I asked him where they were going, he said he did not know. A printer by trade, with a secure home, he was now fleeing for the safety of his family, with only the clothes on their backs and a few items in their hands."

—SYRIAN REFUGEE CRISIS, PERSONAL JOURNAL, OCTOBER 30, 2015

A WORLD OF CATASTROPHE

"Who then is this, that He commands even winds and water, and they obey Him?"

—LUKE 8:25

IN CHAPTER 1, we surveyed some of the catastrophes and disruptive events that occurred at the beginning stages of redemptive history. But what of the things that are yet to come? While it's important to state that no one knows precisely what the future will hold, not only does the Bible speak much about the last days, but there is also much that we can learn by carefully observing the world in which we presently live. It is our opinion that with a careful analysis of what the Scriptures say about things to come, along with a close examination of well-established patterns of history and current global trends, we may gain some clarity concerning what our future holds. In fact, many elements of what we're about to discuss are already unfolding, such as natural and man-made disasters and wars and global conflicts.

BIRTH PAINS

In Jesus' Olivet Discourse—which could also simply be called "Jesus' Sermon on the End Times"—He prophesied concerning the calamities of the last days: "For nation will rise against nation, and kingdom against kingdom, and in various places there will be famines and earthquakes. But all these things are merely the beginning of birth pangs" (Matt. 24:7-8). It's fascinating that Jesus likened the disasters of the last days to birth pains. Throughout his ministry, the Lord consistently used very natural analogies that any common person could understand. As a rule, the nature of birth pains are fairly consistent. They start relatively mild and then gradually increase in both frequency and intensity. Eventually they reach extreme levels of pain, and finally they give way to a baby. Jesus said that the last days would be like this. The birth pains, of course, are the increasingly difficult calamities that will befall the world, whereas the birth is the return of Jesus and the establishment of His kingdom.

EARTHQUAKES

It is fascinating to note that among all other kinds of calamities, Jesus specifically highlighted earthquakes. This was not something new that Jesus introduced. Rather it has very clear precedence among the biblical prophets. As the Lord spoke long ago through the prophet Haggai:

> For thus says the LORD of hosts, 'Once more in a little while, I am going to shake the heavens and the earth, the sea also and the dry land. I will shake all the nations. . . . I am going to shake the heavens and the earth. I will overthrow the thrones of kingdoms and destroy the power of the kingdoms of the nations. (Haggai 2:6-7, 21-22)

Beyond the many earthquakes that will define the last days, the Scriptures also say that when Jesus actually returns, the earth will experience an unparalleled earthquake. The prophet Zechariah says this earthquake will actually result in a transformation of the very topography of Jerusalem:

In that day His feet will stand on the Mount of Olives, which is in front of Jerusalem on the east; and the Mount of Olives will be split in the middle from east to west by a large valley, so that half of the mountain will move toward the north and the other half toward the south. (Zechariah 14:4)

It will be so intense in fact that it will devastate the entire earth:

Then there came flashes of lightning, rumblings, peals of thunder and a severe earthquake. No earthquake like it has ever occurred since mankind has been on earth, so tremendous was the quake. (Revelation 16:18)

NATURAL DISASTERS

Jesus specifically warned us that the period before His return would be defined by catastrophes and disasters following the pattern of birth pains. They would gradually increase in both frequency and intensity. Can we find any direct evidence that both natural and man-made disasters are increasing right now? The answer is most certainly yes. Why is this important? While no man knows the day or the hour of Christ's return, Jesus Himself told His disciples that we can indeed know the season of His return. "Learn the parable from the fig tree," He said. "When its branch has already become tender and puts forth its leaves, you know that summer is near; so, you too, when you see all these things, recognize that He is near, right at the door" (Matt. 24:32-33). So there are things that we will be able to observe in the earth that will indicate that His return is very close. To be clear, just a few verses later, He also warned against setting dates for His return (v. 36), but in no way does this conflict with discerning the *season* of His return. Jesus was not ambiguous about this matter. He actually commanded those of us who are His followers to, *know* when His return is near, specifically when we see the dramatic increase in all the things that He mentioned (v. 33). What then are the things that Jesus was speaking about? Let's begin with the natural disasters.

Today there is a raging debate concerning "climate change." The debate centers around whether or not mankind's impact on the planet is causing negative global climate change. Those on the political Left seem convinced that this is the case, most often blaming the Western world. Those on the Right tend to say that such claims are an excuse to levy heavy financial penalties on American companies and individuals for doing just about anything, all in the name of saving the planet. Regardless as to where one stands on the debate, the fact is that there is verifiable climate change taking place. Whether or not mankind is causing it, or if we are simply experiencing normal long-term cyclical planetary weather patterns is not at all the point here. The fact is that natural disasters are increasing and happening more frequently.

In 2015, The Center for Research on the Epidemiology of Disasters (CRED), the world's foremost agency for the study of public health during mass emergencies, published a report called "The Human Cost of Weather Related Disasters." The CRED's Emergency Events Database (EM-DAT) "contains the world's most comprehensive data on the occurrence and effects of more than 21,000 technological and natural disasters from 1900 to the present day."[1] The report analyzed natural disasters from 1995-2015 and compared them to previous periods. The report shows that natural disasters are occurring now almost twice as frequently as they were twenty years ago, and all signs are that they will continue to increase. "While scientists cannot calculate what percentage of this rise is due to climate change, predictions of more extreme weather in the future almost certainly mean that we will witness a continued upward trend in weather-related disasters in the decades ahead," the report said.[2] According to Debarati Guha-Sapir, professor at CRED, "All we can say is that certain disaster types are increasing. Floods are definitely increasing."[3]

The United States federal government's National Oceanic and Atmospheric Administration (NOAA) maintains a website that lists every disaster in the United States that has cost over a billion dollars, going back to 1980.[4] The site actually lists the dates, locations, number of deaths, and of course, the total cost of damages for every event. What does the data tell us? First, it clearly shows that large-scale (billion dollars and up) natural disasters in the United States have been drastically increasing over the past forty years. Throughout the 1980s, it lists an average of 2.7 large-scale natural disasters per year. In the 1990s, the average had increased to 4.6. During the first decade of the 2000s, the average had increased to 5.4. The current decade, though not yet complete at the time of this writing, is currently at 12.14 per year on average.

Two thousand seventeen was the most-costly year on record for natural disasters in the United States. Of course, this is only in the United States. In 2017 there were 710 natural catastrophes globally. Globally speaking, the data clearly shows that natural disasters are increasing in both frequency and intensity.[5] There has been a 400 percent spike in global weather-related catastrophes since 1970.[6]

So the pattern that we were told to look for is most certainly here. Of all the things to look for, Jesus specifically said that the period before His return would be defined by, among other things, a notable increase in weather-related catastrophes. This is precisely what we are experiencing in our day. The question, however, is whether or not the church is paying attention.

WARS AND RUMORS OF WARS

We've discussed natural disasters, but what about man-made disasters? As Jesus listed the specific things that the final generation before His return will witness, he also specifically mentioned warfare and various forms of national and ethnic conflict. In fact, this was the first issue that he highlighted. Jesus foretold that, "nation will rise against nation, and kingdom against kingdom" (Matt. 24:7).

When we think of warfare, most immediately think of one particular nation invading or attacking another nation. We think of things like Nebuchadnezzar invading Israel or Nazi Germany's invasion of Poland or France in World War II. This kind of conflict would fall under the category of "kingdom against kingdom." There can be no question that these kinds of *international* conflicts will be common in the last days.

Jesus' previous reference to "nation against nation," (v. 7) however, is often misunderstood or overlooked by many Christians. The term used for nation is the Greek word *ethnos,* from which we derive the English word *ethnic* or *ethnicity*. As common as traditional international warfare will be in the days ahead, we could argue that it will be the many *intranational* conflicts that will be equally devastating. With the rise of identity politics, there can be little doubt that the world will see an increase in sectarian conflicts between peoples who differ ethnically, politically, socially and/or religiously, yet who reside within the same sovereign political borders. Today, such conflicts are exploding across the earth. According to Jerry Z. Muller, professor of history at the Catholic University of America, ethnic nationalism "will continue to shape the world in the twenty-first century."[7]

Of the roughly sixty ongoing armed conflicts taking place in the world at the time of this writing, only one is between sovereign nation-states. The other fifty-nine are interstate, intrastate or non-state conflicts.[8] Closely related to the increase of ethnic conflict is what some have described as *identity warfare* or iWar. Identity warfare is fighting by groups without any common national identity for a common cause, such as ISIS or Al-Qaeda. This type of warfare is more likely rooted in religious conflict. There can be little question that this will be one of the most common forms of warfare in the days ahead. We are already seeing its dramatic increase in our day.

In his book *The Rise of iWar* Col. Glenn J. Voelz says that iWar is characterized by three distinct elements: Individualization, Identity and Information. He says, "These pillars provide a conceptual framework for analyzing the dramatic changes in doctrine, technology, and strategic focus that have redefined how the United States wages war abroad and protects its borders at home." Concerning the phenomena of Individualization, he goes on to say:

> Over the last decade, the U.S. national security apparatus shifted
> from its traditional focus on conventional military adversaries to an
> emphasis on nonstate threats and opponents fighting as dispersed,

highly adaptive networks. This reorientation led to the adoption of new analytical methods and operational approaches based on the symmetric disaggression of threats down to the lowest possible level—often the individual combatant.[9]

While symmetrical warfare between various nation-states has seen a significant decrease over the past seventy years, asymmetrical, cyber, sectarian, and iWarfare has risen sharply. So, when considering Jesus' words concerning the rise of "wars and rumors of wars," we must understand His warning to apply to a much broader definition of war than is commonly understood.

Syria is a perfect example of what the future may hold. Over the past several years, what began as an intrastate conflict or civil war has developed into a powerful magnet for local, regional, and global powers, who have all amassed there. At present, there are military forces in Syria from every single one of the permanent members of the UN Security Council. These are not nations representing UN peace keeping forces but are independent sovereign powers who are there for their own military, political, or national security interests. Beyond the United States, Russia, Great Britain, France, and China, there is also a strong Turkish, Iranian, Syrian, Saudi Arabian, and Qatari military presence there.

Beyond all of the international powers, there are also numerous militant groups from within the country. The BBC has reported that there are as many as a thousand different armed opposition groups in Syria with more than 100,000 fighters.[10] What began as a series of simple sectarian driven protests led by Syrian Sunni Muslims against the Syrian Alawaite-led government has spiraled out of control, leaving more than half a million people dead. Further this conflict now threatens to spread to the surrounding region and possibly spark a larger global war. Many worry that it will lead to a World War III. Veteran foreign-affairs journalist Joe Lauria, in an article titled, "Risking WWIII in Syria" lists numerous historical wars that have been fought in Syria. Then he concludes:

We may be now looking at an epic war with similar historical significance. All these previous battles, as momentous as they were, were regional in nature. What we are potentially facing is a war that goes beyond the Soviet-U.S. proxy wars of the Cold War era, and beyond the proxy war that has so far taken place in the five-year Syrian civil war. Russia is already present in Syria. The entry of the United States and its allies would risk a direct confrontation between the two largest nuclear powers on earth.[11]

Perhaps unbeknownst to Lauria, his words may be entirely prophetic.

CONCLUSION

We have seen that both natural and man-made disasters are increasing. Jesus warned us that this is exactly what would happen as we draw nearer to the time of the great tribulation and His return to earth. He commanded us to learn the lesson of the fig tree and recognize that when we see all of these things, then we are to know that His return is drawing near. Sadly, even within the church, there will be those who claim that this information means absolutely nothing and that Christians should pay no attention. For those believers, however, who do take Jesus' words at face value and who are watching the specific signs that Jesus spoke of, the evidence is there. The contractions are increasing. There is a birth coming. Believers must begin to be prepared. The writer of Hebrews reinforced that theme:

> See to it that you do not refuse Him who is speaking. For if those did not escape when they refused him who warned them on earth, much less will we escape who turn away from Him who warns from heaven. And His voice shook the earth then, but now He has promised, saying, "Yet once more I will shake not only the earth, but also the heaven." . . . Therefore, since we receive a kingdom which cannot be shaken, let us show gratitude, by which we may offer to God an acceptable service with reverence and awe; for our God is a consuming fire. (Hebrews 12:25-29)

"The house where we stayed was the sleeping quarters and a weapons armory for ISIS until just six months before we arrived. It was surreal. Each morning and evening we would hear the bombing nearby in Mosul, which provided us a constant reminder that we were still in the war zone, and that the enemy had been driven back only several kilometers. At night, as I lay in my cot, most likely in the same room where ISIS fighters had also slept just months before, the realization of where we were brought a soberness of mind that I needed. This was not a Jason Bourne movie. It was real. We were not actors in a motion picture thriller. Although it was only brief, we were participants in an unfolding humanitarian crisis where the lives of thousands had been destroyed, including many Yezidis who had been beheaded and taken as sex slaves by ISIS."

—KURDISTAN REFUGEE CRISIS, PERSONAL JOURNAL, MAY 6, 2017

THE LAST REICH

After this I kept looking in the night visions, and behold, a fourth beast, dreadful and terrifying and extremely strong; and it had large iron teeth. It devoured and crushed and trampled down the remainder with its feet.

—DANIEL 7:7

AS WE SAW in the last chapter, the last days will be defined by an increase in natural and man-made disasters. Among these, the greatest and most emphasized disaster of the future, the most disruptive, destructive, and thus relevant, will be global conflict sparked by the rise of radical Islam. In order to understand why I can so confidently make this statement, we must begin by understanding what the Bible says about the greatest catastrophe that the world will ever witness.

THE FINAL DICTATOR AND THE GREAT TRIBULATION
According to the Scriptures, as the world approaches the return of Jesus, it will increasingly experience great tribulation, which Jesus likens to

"birth pains" (see Matt. 24:8). Although this period of great trouble will be defined by both natural and man-made disasters, the worst of these catastrophes will be caused by a great dictator popularly known as the "Antichrist" (1 John 2:18-22).

The Bible teaches that this individual will successfully extend his authority over a coalition of nations and will seek to conquer many other nations (see Dan. 7:7, 20, 24-25; 11:36-45; Rev. 13:1; 17:3, 7, 12, 16). The reign of terror brought upon the world by the Antichrist and his coalition of nations will result in the greatest tribulation the world has ever known. The Bible likens this coming multi-national alliance or empire to a metaphorical beast, that is "exceedingly dreadful, with its teeth of iron and its claws of bronze, and which devoured, crushed and trampled down the remainder with its feet" (Dan. 7:19). The military might of this coming empire will appear to be beyond challenge so that the people of the earth will fearfully ask, "Who is like the beast, and who is able to wage war with him?" (Rev. 13:4).

During the early phase of his career, we are told that the Antichrist will invade many nations (see Dan. 11:41) sparking a final world war. Daniel the prophet even seems to indicate that the Antichrist will attack the most powerful nation in the world, stating, "He will take action against the strongest of fortresses" (Dan. 11:39). Ultimately, we are told that he will attain, "authority over every tribe and people and tongue and nation" (Rev. 13:7). The Scriptures soberly declare that, "he will destroy to an extraordinary degree" (Dan. 8:24). Of this exceedingly dark future, the prophet Daniel says, "there will be a time of distress such as never occurred since there was a nation until that time." (Dan. 12:1). Building upon Daniel's warning, Jesus Himself reiterated, "For then there will be a great tribulation, such as has not occurred since the beginning of the world until now, nor ever will. Unless those days had been cut short, no life would have been saved; but for the sake of the elect those days will be cut short" (Matt. 24:21-22).

It is important to note that the primary target of the Antichrist and his military machine will be the state of Israel, the Jewish people, and Christians. Seeing this future time in a vision, Daniel spoke of the coming dictator, "waging war with the saints and overpowering them" (Dan. 7:21). The apostle John reiterates this in the book of Revelation, stating that it was given to the Antichrist "to make war with the saints and to overcome them" (Rev. 13:7). Specifically, we are warned that the Antichrist will make his target, "those who keep the commandments of God and hold to the testimony of Jesus" (Rev. 12:17).

THE GLOBAL RISE OF RADICAL ISLAM

In the context of a prophetic unparalleled tribulation aimed specifically at Israel, the Jewish people, and Christians, let us consider the reality presently on the ground. In November 2017, the Catholic organization Aid to the Church in Need published a study in which they concluded that the persecution of Christians across the world is worse, "than at any time in history." According to the report, "Not only are Christians more persecuted than any other faith group, but ever-increasing numbers are experiencing the very worst forms of persecution."[1] The report specifically studied the dire conditions of Christians living in the nations of China, Egypt, Eritrea, India, Iran, Iraq, Nigeria, North Korea, Pakistan, Saudi Arabia, Sudan, Syria and Turkey over the period lasting from 2015 until 2017. The report also placed specific emphasis on Iraq and Syria, where it argued that if not for direct military action and the assistance of various Christian aid organizations, Christians there would cease to exist.

Another report, the 2018 World Watch List (WWL) released by Open Doors concluded that, "Approximately 215 million Christians now experience high, very high, or extreme levels of persecution."[2] Although the fifty most dangerous nations for Christians did include ten non-Muslims majority nations such as North Korea, (which has over fifty thousand people in prison camps), the vast majority of nations on the list were Muslim majority nations. These included Middle Eastern nations, as well as African and Asian nations.

In other words, although Christian persecution is by no means limited to Muslim majority nations, there is clearly a direct correlation between the dramatic rise of Christian persecution globally and Islam. For those who understand the biblical testimony, and who have been following the predictions of various futurists for the past few decades, this shouldn't come as a surprise.

Although such a comment may upset some readers, the Western world and the Islamic world are presently in the early stages of a prolonged and bloody cultural clash. This clash—this great catastrophe—will continue to increase in both its destructiveness and intensity until Jesus returns. As the legendary Harvard professor Samuel Huntington predicted over twenty-five years ago, "The fault lines between civilizations are becoming the central lines of conflict in global politics." The days ahead will increasingly be defined by the clash between "Western arrogance," and "Islamic intolerance." And in what would become one of his most famous quotes, Huntington rightly observed, "Islam's borders are bloody and so are its innards. . . . The underlying problem for the West is not Islamic fundamentalism. It is Islam, a different civilization whose people are convinced of the superiority of their culture and are obsessed with the inferiority of their power."[3] Indeed, we are presently in the early stages of this collision of two very different civilizations that Huntington so accurately predicted a quarter century ago. History informs us that it is the first few hundred years of any such conflict that are always the bloodiest. If the early decades of this clash are any indicator, this time will be no different.

Let's begin with some simple acknowledgment of current demographic trends and then we'll discuss some basic history to contextualize our predictions.

MUSLIM GROWTH AND DEMOGRAPHICS

According to a comprehensive survey released by the Pew Research Center in 2017, there are presently over "1.8 billion Muslims in the world as of 2015." This is roughly a quarter of the entire global population. Although Islam is the second largest religion after Christianity, it is the fastest growing. If current demographic trends continue, within the next eighty years, Muslims will outnumber Christians, making Islam the world's largest religion.[4]

Although Muslim populations are dramatically expanding in parts of the world that have not historically been considered Muslim, such as Europe, Russia, and large portions of the African continent, Islam will continue to dominate the epicenter of the biblical world—the Middle East. The point here is very simple; until Jesus returns, not only is Islam not going away, it is likely to emerge as the planet's most common and dominant religious force.

ISLAM: A RELIGION OF PEACE?

We know Islam is a big religion in terms of number of followers, but why should we expect a violent clash between Islam and the rest of the world? It is simply because Islam is fundamentally and irreparably a religion of violence and intolerance. From its very inception, it has always been such. Whether we look to the Qur'an and Islam's other earliest sacred texts or the examples left behind by Muhammad, the founder of Islam, and his earliest followers, all of these sources are rife with violence, intolerance, and calls to those who follow Islam to continue this horrific legacy.

In 2014, when the radical Sunni group known as ISIS suddenly burst out of Syria into central and northern Iraq, many were shocked at the unchecked barbarity of this group. Not only were the soldiers of the new caliphate reckless in their bloodlust, they were brazen, even proud of their utter disregard for human life. Mass executions were filmed and sent to major news organizations around the world. Beyond the public beheadings, entire villages and towns were massacred and cast into mass graves. People were thrown alive off the tops of buildings. Others were locked into steel cages, doused with gasoline, and burnt alive. Others yet were bound and slowly lowered into pools to be killed in the most slow, calculated, and cruel manner imaginable. In one case, a group of children were literally sawn in half with chainsaws. Beyond all this, there was the deliberate enslavement of tens of thousands of young girls as sex slaves. As all of this dominated the news cycle, the West was debating whether or not all of this barbarism was genuinely "Islamic" or not. The debate was rather polarized. Some essentially said that ISIS has nothing to do with Islam while others said the soldiers of ISIS are the truest of Muslims.

So what is the truth? Is Islam in fact a "religion of peace" as many of its proponents and defenders claim? Or is it a religion founded upon violent imperialism, as many of its critics claim? The answer to these questions will dramatically affect the kind of future we may expect to witness. The answer of course to these questions can only be found by examining the life of Islam's founder and "prophet" Muhammad, it's holy book, the Qur'an, as well the lives of the first Muslims. Was the unchecked savagery of ISIS in keeping with the teaching and example left behind by Muhammad and his earliest disciples? If this can be proven, then we may absolutely expect to see much more Islamic terrorism in the future. We must understand that if Islam's very foundations promote both violence and intolerance toward all who are not Muslims, then the predictable ramifications for the future are very dark. Although much of the world doesn't want to hear the truth concerning this matter, when we take an honest look at the life and example of Muhammad, as well as his earliest, "rightly guided" successors, they both bear a striking resemblance to the brutal face of ISIS. Even the briefest survey of early Islamic history and sacred documents shows this to be the case.

MUHAMMAD: PROPHET OF CONQUEST

When I hear various commentators and apologists make the claim that Islam is, at its core, a religion of peace, I'm bewildered. Nobody who honestly examines Muhammad's life, the Qur'an, or the horror of the early Muslim conquests could arrive at this conclusion. Under Muhammad's leadership, the Muslims carried out approximately eighty military expeditions.[5] These ranged from events as small as attacking a caravan to decimating entire towns. Let's consider one of the worst examples. In the year AD 627, only five years after Muhammad began his so-called prophetic career, he personally oversaw what can only honestly be called a mass slaughter. Muhammad and his soldiers laid siege to the large Jewish village of Qurayzah. After twenty-five days, the villagers surrendered, hoping that Muhammad would be merciful. Instead, Muhammad ordered his men to dig several trenches and forced several hundred of the men from Qurayzah to walk into them. Upon Muhammad's orders, every last man was beheaded. The trenches became mass graves. From Ibn Ishaq's *Sirat Rasul*, Islam's earliest and most well received biography of Muhammad, we read the gruesome account:

> Then they surrendered and the apostle confined them. . . . Then the apostle went out to the market of Medina (which is still its market today) and dug trenches in it. Then he sent for them and struck off their heads in those trenches as they were brought out to him in batches. . . . They were 600 or 700 in all, though some put the figures as high as 800 or 900. . . . This went on until the apostle made an end to them.[6]

The village was plundered, and the woman and children were taken as concubines or slaves. This story is virtually identical to what the world witnessed when ISIS unleashed its reign of terror in Iraq and Syria. Perhaps those who declared that ISIS had nothing to do with Islam were thinking wishfully, but they were not thinking logically or from a historical perspective. Even if this brutal episode were a one-off incident in Muhammad's life, it wouldn't diminish his brutality, which is essential to understand because according to Islamic theology whatever Muhammad said or did is to be emulated. Because Islam casts Muhammad as "the perfect man," whatever he said, did, forbid, or condoned becomes the very pattern for every Muslim to follow. Ninety-one times throughout the Qur'an, Muslims are told to imitate Muhammad. In Quran 3:31, for example, Muhammad declares, "If you love Allah, then follow me."[7]

THE QUR'AN: THE BOOK OF ISLAMIC CONQUEST

Despite the mantra heard throughout the West that Islam is a peaceful religion, and more than clear for anyone who actually reads the Qur'an and the hadith (Islamic sacred traditions), there are hundreds of instances where Muslims are commanded to engage in militant violence against unbelievers for the purpose of Islamic dominance. In one well-known tradition, Muhammad declared, "I have been ordered to fight the people till they say: 'None has the right to be worshipped but Allah.'"[8] Elsewhere, in the Qur'an, we read:

> Fight those who believe not in Allah nor the Last Day, nor hold that forbidden which hath been forbidden by Allah and His Messenger, nor acknowledge the religion of Truth, (even if they are) of the People of the Book, until they pay the Jizya with willing submission, and feel themselves subdued. (Qur'an 9:29)

Some make the claim that this passage only applied to a particular time in Muhammad's career but was not intended to be carried on today. This was never the understanding by Muhammad or his earliest successors. Ibn Kathir, the most widely respected early commentator on the Qur'an states that the early Muslim conquests were specifically carried out as a direct result of obedience to this particular qur'anic injunction. From Ibn Kathir's commentary on Qur'an 9:29, we read the following:

> Allah commands the believers to fight the disbelievers, the closest in area to the Islamic state, then the farthest. This is why the Messenger of Allah started fighting the idolaters in the Arabian Peninsula. When he finished with them... He then started fighting the People of the Scriptures.

When Ibn Kathir wrote "People of the Scriptures," he was referring to Jews and Christians. The conclusion is unavoidable. Muhammad established the pattern. The expansion of Islam would be accomplished through warfare, specifically against the pagans, and then against Jews and Christians. Modern Muslims who similarly use violence to further the cause of Islam are not expressing some aberration of Islam, rather they are imitating Muhammad himself.

THE EARLY MUSLIM CONQUESTS

After Muhammad's death, his closest friends and disciples assumed leadership over the Muslim community and dramatically expanded what their leader had started. Robert Hoyland is professor of late antique and early Islamic Middle Eastern history at New York University's Institute for the Study of the Ancient World. He has written several books on Arabs and the rise of Islam. His doctoral thesis was on non-Muslim accounts of the rise of Islam. He reminds us that the great conquest of the Middle East was envisioned by Muhammad himself. That he "initiated this war effort, campaigning north in the direction of Syria, is clearly stated by Muslim and non-Muslim writers." Hoyland describes, "the first caliphs as extending [Muhammad's] policy, effectively running a 'jihad state,' . . . whose overriding aim was the expansion of the state in the name of God."[9] Ibn Kathir summarizes this initial period of Islamic conquest:

> After Muhammad's death, his executor, friend, and Caliph, Abu Bakr, became the leader... On behalf of the Prophet, Abu Bakr... started preparing the Islamic armies to fight the Roman cross worshippers, and the Persian fire worshippers. By the blessing of his mission, Allah opened the lands for him and brought down Caesar and Kisra and those who obeyed them among the servants. Abu Bakr spent their treasures in the cause of Allah, just as the Messenger of Allah had foretold would happen. This mission continued after Abu Bakr at the hands of he whom Abu Bakr chose to be his successor... Umar bin Al-Khattab. With Umar, Allah humiliated the disbelievers, suppressed the tyrants and hypocrites, and opened the eastern and western parts of the world. The treasures of various countries were brought to Umar from near and far provinces, and he divided them

according to the legitimate and accepted method… During Uthman's reign, Islam wore its widest garment and Allah's unequivocal proof was established in various parts of the world over the necks of the servants. Islam appeared in the eastern and western parts of the world and Allah's Word was elevated and His religion apparent. The pure religion reached its deepest aims against Allah's enemies, and whenever Muslims overcame a community, they moved to the next one, and then the next one, crushing the tyrannical evil doers. They did this in reverence to Allah's statement, O you who believe! Fight those of the disbelievers who are close to you.[10]

You will find the same story in any early Islamic history you consult. In these earliest Muslim accounts, we find detailed descriptions of battle after battle, slaughter after slaughter carried out by Muhammad's successors. As Ibn Kathir states above, the early Muslims viewed the success of their bloody conquests as a direct sign of Allah's endorsement of their mission. The more dead bodies, the more bloodshed, the greater was the victory.

The first of Muhammad's successors was his best friend Abu Bakr. Abu Bakr's general was Khalid bin al-Walid who had also fought under the leadership of Muhammad. Under Muhammad, Khalid fought so effectively that he earned the title *The Sword of Allah*. Upon Abu Bakr's orders, in AD 633-634, Khalid extended an invitation to the people of Persia to accept Islam. In truth, this "invitation" was nothing more than a direct threat: Accept Islam or die. The actual invitation read as follows:

> In the name of Allah, the Compassionate, the Merciful. From Khalid bin al-Walid to the governors of Persia. Embrace Islam so that you may be safe. If not, make a covenant with me and pay the Jizyah tax. Otherwise, I have brought you a people who love death just as you love drinking wine.

In al-Tabari's book *History*, we are given much more detail regarding what unfolded when the Persians rejected al-Walid's "invitation."

Tabari recalls, "The unbelievers started fleeing right and left. . . . Only an insignificant number got away. That day God killed one hundred thousand of them. The whole clearing was covered with corpses, in all directions."[11] In another significant victory over the Byzantine Romans, al-Waqidi recounts: "The Romans displayed great patience but lost nerve at sunset. They fled, followed by the Muslims who captured or killed as they pleased. About 100,000 Romans were killed, a similar amount was captured and a similar amount drowned in an-Naqusah Creek." Elsewhere al-Waqidi, records Caliph Abu Bakr's words as he appealed to the Muslims to attack Syria:

> All Praise to Allah alone and salutations to His Messenger. Know that I intend sending an army to Syria to expel the Disbelievers and those who do not tread the straight path from there. Whoever amongst you intends to wage Jihad should hasten to obey Allah and make preparations for Allah says: "Go forth lightly armed or heavily armed and wage Jihad with your wealth and lives in the path of Allah." (Qur'an 9:41)

Jewish historian Bat Ye'or recounts the Muslim conquest of the region that is now the Gaza strip and Israel: "Consequently, the whole Gaza region up to Caesarea was sacked and devastated in the [Syrian] campaign of 634. Four thousand Jewish, Christian, and Samaritan peasants who defended their land were massacred."[12]

All in all, the numbers killed by the early "rightly guided" successors of Muhammad are staggering. Within one hundred years, 50 percent of global Christianity had come under Islamic subjugation. Though Christianity has survived in that part of the world, it has done so as a struggling—and shrinking—minority.

As we consider the brutal nature of early Islamic conquests and the vast numbers killed, we are confronted with a terrifying but undeniable fact: Rather than representing an aberration or perversion of true Islam, modern jihadist groups such as ISIS or Al-Qaeda are actually carrying on the tradition of conquest that began with Muhammad in Arabia and continued under his successors. As Samuel Huntington rightly stated, some "have argued that the West does not have problems with Islam but only with violent Islamist extremists. Fourteen hundred years of history demonstrate otherwise."[13] This then, is the first reason why we may rightly expect the clash between Islam and the rest of the world to continue to expand until Jesus returns.

THE RISE OF SALAFISM AND WAHABBISM

The second reason why we should expect an expanding worldwide conflict with Islam is because of the simple fact that violent radical Islamic ideology itself is currently spreading across the globe like wildfire. We must be very clear to stress that the vast majority of Muslims throughout the world do not subscribe to the violence and brutality of Muhammad, ISIS, or other modern jihadist groups. Many Muslims are quite ignorant of their own history and few actually study the Qur'an in their own language. Beyond this, Islam is far from monolithic. The Islam taught and practiced in Iran is vastly different than the Islam in Saudi Arabia or northern Iraq or in Turkey. Islam indeed comes in many forms, and Muslims are as different as Christians are different. That said, over the past several decades there has been a global campaign pushing a particular form of Islam that most refer to as Salafism or Wahhabism. Not only does this more radical form of Islam find its origins in Saudi Arabia, but its dramatic expansion throughout the world has been funded by the Saudis. In fact, this Saudi program to spread Salafism throughout the world has been the single greatest, most well-funded campaign to spread an ideology in the history of mankind. In testimony before the US House Committee on Oversight and Government Reform in 2005, former CIA Director James Woolsey stated that "Estimates of the amount spent by the Saudis in the last 30 years spreading Wahhabi beliefs throughout the world vary from $70 billion to $100 billion."[14] And according to Yousaf Butt, visiting senior research fellow at the Center for Technology and National Security Policy at the National Defense University:

Exact numbers are not known, but it is thought that more than $100 billion have been spent on exporting fanatical Wahhabism to various much poorer Muslim nations worldwide over the past three decades. It might well be twice that number. By comparison, the Soviets spent about $7 billion spreading communism worldwide in the 70 years from 1921 to 1991.[15]

This spending has not let up. If we include the last decade, then the rough estimate of the money dished out by the Saudi Royal Family over the past forty years to spread Wahhabi Islam around the world is roughly $150 billion. This is absolutely stunning. Over the past forty years, a single family outspent the combined total spending of all Christians globally for the spread of the gospel. That the world is seeing a drastic rise in fundamentalist Islam, terrorism, and most specifically, violent, militant Islamic organizations is absolutely no mystery whatso-ever. Saudi Arabia has funded the single greatest religious propaganda campaign in the history of mankind. They have been wildly successful. Who can doubt the success of Saudis' effort to spread Wahhabism around the world? Who can doubt that a movement has begun. The out-of-control snowball has turned into an avalanche and is showing no signs of slowing down. Over the past few decades, across the globe, among the expanding ocean of Muslim youths, jihad has increasingly become more fashionable by the year. Pandora's box has been ripped wide open, and the world is only now beginning to feel the wrath of this horrific reality.

Let's consider the number of ISIS recruits from around the world. As far back as 2015, within only the first year of the establishment of the Caliphate in Syria and Iraq, roughly thirty thousand foreign fighters had left home to join the Caliphate. Of those recruited, roughly 78 percent were young people. More than 4,500 came from Western countries, including 250 Americans and 750 Britons.[16] Compare this to the vast number of young people in the West who are leaving the church as they reach adulthood. Present statistics hold that in the United States, a majority of those raised in church stop attending when they reach adulthood.[17] As youth pastors throughout the West are utilizing every form of entertainment imaginable to keep kids involved in church, the ISIS Caliphate called young people to abandon everything, burn their passports, and likely come die for the cause. Unlike the majority of Christian youth pastors, however, ISIS was wildly successful. There is something profoundly seductive to the radical call of jihad that many Western analysts still have not fully grasped. Imagine the pride many young men and women feel when they sign up to join the military, particularly during times of national crisis. In the United States, just after 9/11, many young Americans flocked to the recruiting stations, eager to show their love for their nation. Imagine the pride and excitement that many young people feel when they decide to go to seminary or some kind of missions training program to prepare themselves for a life serving the Lord. Add to that the camaraderie that many youths find when they join street gangs. Combine all of these together and we may begin to understand how many of these young jihadis feel when they decide to leave everything behind to join the Caliphate. Analysts would be foolish to underestimate the power of the growing jihadist movement.

BLOWBACK AND MUSLIM MARTYR CULTURE

The third reason we are right to expect a global clash of civilizations is because of the dynamic of *blowback*. Faced with the growing problem of Islamic terrorism, global leaders are quite naturally wrestling through possible solutions to this global crisis. Most conservatives follow the line of conventional wisdom that holds the only way to defeat any particular militant group or movement is to simply crush it with a decisive series of heavy-handed, military blows. While this approach may be effective against the vast majority of militant groups, in the case of religious movements with a theology of martyrdom, such traditional thinking doesn't always hold true. As the third-century Christian theologian Tertullian famously noted, "We multiply whenever we are mown down by you; the blood of the martyrs is the seed of the church."[18] His rationale was simple; as martyrs courageously die for the cause, observers are often converted while the surviving faithful are strengthened in their commitment. Today, vast segments of modern Christianity have lost touch with the value that the early church placed on martyrdom as foundational to its witness. Islam, on the other hand, has maintained its own rich tradition of martyrdom, which is as vibrant today as at its inception. Of course, there are some significant differences between Christian and Islamic martyrdom that must be noted. Whereas Christian martyrdom consists in laying down one's life to save another, or in dying at the hands of persecutors or oppressive worldly governments, Islamic martyrdom consists in actually dying in battle seeking to destroy non-Muslims and all non-Muslim worldly systems. Whereas Christian martyrdom is modeled after the pattern of Jesus, who actually prayed for the forgiveness of his executioners, the Islamic martyr is viewed as more of a Davidic character, valiantly risking his life fighting Goliath, the mighty heathen. To the Muslim jihadi then, the bigger and more powerful the military power, the more valorous it is to die fighting them. Cutting against conventional wisdom therefore, the more decisive and heavy-handed these military superpowers become, the more opportunity to become a martyr-hero. Rather than eliminating Islamic radicalism, traditional military responses often actually inspire waves of young jihadis to take up the cause. Certainly the first two decades of the twenty-first century have proven this to be true. Wave after wave, new recruits keep coming. With several of the most populous Muslim nations in the world having over half of their populations younger than twenty-five, there is a near bottomless pool of potential recruits for the expanding global jihad.

There is another dynamic at play that makes defeating Islamic militancy nearly impossible. Most outside observers cannot understand why Palestinian terrorists deliberately place their fellow Palestinians in harm's way. Don't the terrorists realize that this will turn the hearts of their own people against them? It would seem as though they are following the worst possible strategy. The reality, however, is that they actually have a much better understanding of the various psychological dynamics of warfare than we give them credit for. Jihadi strategists actually target innocent Israeli civilians hoping to bring a harsh response from Israel. They actually yearn for the Israelis to respond with a heavy hand. Terrorists actually want otherwise moderate Muslims to suffer. The ongoing cycles of terror and repression make it very difficult, if not impossible, for anyone to remain neutral or moderate. The purpose of Palestinian terror is to increase polarization within Palestinian society.

What is happening in the Palestinian regions of Israel is but a microcosm of what is happening across the globe. The Al-Qaeda or ISIS strategists are very well aware of how blowback works. When terrorists attack innocent people at a Christmas market in some European city, for example, they hope that Europeans will actually turn their rage against moderate Muslims. There is nothing that the subversive jihadis would like to see more. If moderate Muslims are unfairly attacked, this will further incite angry reactions and the radicalization of the larger Muslim population. Jihadists purposefully stoke the flames of the emerging cultural inferno. Remember, at the core of Islamic terrorism is the goal of utterly destroying the current system, the present order.

Islamic terrorists are driven by their apocalyptic narrative. First comes chaos, then Allah will bring deliverance, and a new order will emerge from the ashes. The reality is this: The more determined the Western world is to defeat radicalism through militancy, the more that Islamic radicalism tends to grow. In this sense, combatting Islamic jihad is entirely different than conventional war. Philip Jenkins, distinguished professor of history at Baylor and one of the world's leading religion scholars, articulates this dynamic quite well: "terrorism operates on a logic quite different from that of most conventional politics and law enforcement, and concepts like defeat and victory must be understood quite differently from in a regular war."[19]

CONCLUSION

In today's world, where the de facto religion of the age is pluralism, there is an increasing fear to speak critically regarding any religion (other than Christianity). It is difficult for most of us to come to terms with the reality that Islam, the world's second largest and fastest growing religion, is a fundamentally violent and intolerant system. When we are able to garner the courage to face reality, however, we are confronted with a challenge so great that apart from the return of Jesus, there seems to be little hope. Like the generation that was forced to come to terms with the terrifying implications of who Adolph Hitler was and how evil the Nazi regime truly was, it has fallen upon the shepherds and leaders of this generation to come to terms with what is presently rising right before us. This time it is not the limited and localized threat of Nazi Germany. Rather it is a vast, global religious movement. This is the *Last Reich*. This then is the final great challenge that is about to confront the church, and indeed the whole world—an unprecedented, unparalleled force, unlike anything the world has ever faced.

The wider the door opens for the advancement of the gospel, the greater the opposition will be from the enemies of the cross. How great a door has been opened to me and to you for effective work in reaching the lost. I challenge anyone to give me an example of a larger opening given to us to share Christ with Muslims in modern times. I cannot let up on this. We've got to be jarred and awakened to this unprecedented privilege before us. The enemy is pressing hard to hinder us from doing our utmost to get the message of Jesus Christ to these refugees and migrants streaming across the Balkans into Europe.

—SYRIAN REFUGEE CRISIS, PERSONAL JOURNAL, SEPTEMBER 30, 2015

THE SPIRIT OF ANTICHRIST

But the Spirit explicitly says that in later times some will fall away from the faith,
paying attention to deceitful spirits and doctrines of demons.

—I TIMOTHY 4:1

BEYOND THE RISING TIDAL WAVES of Muslim population growth and radical jihadi culture, there is another glaring reason to see Islam as the primary instrument the Lord will use to bring about the coming great tribulation. Islam aligns perfectly with the biblical descriptions of the coming Antichrist system. Consider how John the apostle described the doctrines of Antichrist:

> Who is the liar but the one who denies that Jesus is the Christ? This is the antichrist, the one who denies the Father and the Son. Whoever denies the Son does not have the Father; the one who confesses the Son has the Father also. (1 John 2:22–23)

> For many deceivers have gone out into the world, those who do not acknowledge Jesus Christ as coming in the flesh. This is the deceiver and the antichrist. (2 John 1:7)

According to John, the Antichrist will deny that Jesus is the Messiah. He will deny that in Jesus, God provided atonement for sins. He will deny that in Jesus, God will intervene to save and deliver both Jews and Christians from the great last days persecution. He will deny that God is indeed a loving father, and a God who has indeed revealed Himself by sending His very heart, His essence, His Son, into the world. Any rejection of these things is a denial of the one, true, living God of the Bible.

THE ANTICHRIST DOCTRINES OF ISLAM

With this backdrop, we must understand that the religion of Islam, more than any other religion, philosophy, or belief system, fulfills the biblical descriptions of the Antichrist spirit. The Qur'an makes as one of its highest priorities the denial of all that the Bible affirms concerning the character of the Lord God of Israel and Jesus the Messiah. The Qur'an denies that God would ever call Himself a Father. It denies that God would ever choose to reveal Himself in any way to mankind. In fact, Islam is a direct polemical response against these essential concepts.

In order to properly understand the Antichrist spirit of Islam, there are two doctrines that must first be understood: the *tawhid* and *shirk*. Tawhid refers to the belief in the absolute oneness of God. It is the strictest expression of unitarian monotheism possible. Holding up the pointer finger is a popular gesture among the soldiers of ISIS and indicates tawhid, the oneness of God. In Islam, God is utterly alone. This is why the Christian doctrine of the Trinity is so offensive. This is where shirk comes in. While adherence to tawhid is the highest and most important belief in Islam, the greatest sin is shirk. In essence, shirk is idolatry. Islamic theology denounces the Christian belief that Jesus is the Son of God as "ascribing partners to God." It is viewed as worshipping multiple gods. Thus many Muslims view essential Christian doctrines, such as believing in the fatherhood of God or the sonship of Jesus as the greatest sins conceivable. Such sentiment comes directly from the Qur'an itself. In Qur'an 5:17, those who say that Christ is divine are said to be blasphemers. In chapter 19:88-92 it is called "a gross blasphemy" that is so horrific that "the heavens are about to shatter, the earth is about to tear asunder, and the mountains are about to crumble. Because they claim that the Most Gracious has begotten a son. It is not befitting the Most Gracious that He should beget a son!" And in Qur'an 9:30, speaking of those who believe in the essential historical Christian doctrine that Jesus is the Son of God, it says, "Allah's curse be on them: how they are deluded away from the Truth!"

Without question then, Islam is a religious system that perfectly embodies the spirit of Antichrist as defined by the Bible. No other religion better aligns with the apostle John's specific descriptions concerning the doctrines of the Antichrist. The Antichrist denies the Father and the Son. Likewise, Islam denies the Father and denies the Son. Of course, there are many other ways in which Islam aligns perfectly with the religious system of the Antichrist as described in the Bible.

THE ISLAMIC PRACTICE OF BEHEADING

The book of Revelation has much to say about the martyrdom of the saints in the last days. In Revelation we are told that many would be killed specifically by being beheaded:

> Then I saw thrones, and they sat on them, and judgment was given to them. And I saw the souls of those who had been beheaded because of their testimony of Jesus and because of the word of God, and those who had not worshiped the beast or his image, and had not received the mark on their forehead and on their hand; and they came to life and reigned with Christ for a thousand years. (Revelation 20:4)

In light of such a clear picture of last days martyrdom, we must ask: what global religious system views itself as a divinely appointed system authorized by God to behead those who refuse to submit? While beheading may have been a common form of execution historically, today there is only one major religious system that practices it. As it says in the Qur'an: "If you encounter the disbelievers in a battle, strike-off their heads" (47:4).[1] Beheading was also a common form of execution utilized by both Muhammad and his early successors, and as we are all well aware, it continues to be used in modern times by fundamentalist Muslims all over the world. This then is another way in which Islam perfectly matches the biblical descriptions of the Antichrist system that will overwhelm significant portions of the world before Jesus returns.

ISLAM'S GOAL OF WORLD DOMINATION

Another significant way in which Islam fits hand in glove with the prophesied system of the Antichrist is in its imperial goals of global domination. The genesis of the Islamic doctrine of global conquest of course began with Muhammad who famously declared:

> I have been commanded to fight the people until they testify that there is no deity worthy of worship except Allah and that Muhammad is the Messenger of Allah, establish the prayer and pay the Zakah.[2]

We've already examined the early years of Islamic conquest after Muhammad died. After Muhammad's death in AD 632, his earliest successors followed in their "prophet's" footsteps by engaging in one of the fiercest and most successful military campaigns in history. Within four years after Muhammad died, over three hundred thousand Christians were murdered. Over the next ten years, Muslims killed a million Christians. They besieged city after city, executing the resisters, distributing the booty, and marching as many as sixty thousand women to Mecca to become sex slaves or concubines. In less than one genera-tion, the ancient heart of Christianity was ripped out by the Muslim invaders. Within one hundred years, 50 percent of global Christianity had come under Islamic subjugation. Though Christians have survived in that part of the world, they have done so only as a struggling—and shrinking—minority. Since 2014, with the horrific devastation brought by ISIS, that struggling minority in the ancient heartland of the early church has once again been drastically reduced.

In the book of Daniel, the prophet describes the empire that would be used by Satan in his ultimate and final act of resistance to the Lord's plans of global redemption. Daniel describes this last-days empire as an unfathomably destructive beast:

> After that, in my vision at night I looked, and there before me was a fourth beast—terrifying and frightening and very powerful. It had large iron teeth; it crushed and devoured its victims and trampled underfoot whatever was left. . . . The fourth beast is a fourth kingdom that will appear on earth. It will be different from all the other kingdoms and will devour the whole earth, trampling it down and crushing it. (Daniel 7:7, 23, NIV)

The Bible describes the coming system of the Antichrist as being much more than a mere religious system. It will also be an imperial force bent on expansion, conquering and subjugating "the whole earth." Truly if any religious empire could be described as a beast that "crushed and devoured its victims and trampled underfoot whatever was left," it is Islam. Daniel's description could not more perfectly describe Islam in its historical expansion out of Arabia and into the whole world. From Africa to Europe, from Syria to the Philippines, across the globe the iron-toothed beast of Islam continues its long historical program of gradually crushing and devouring virtually every non-Muslim culture and people that it comes in contact with.

THE POWER OF ISLAMIC PROPHECY

The next significant factor that increases the likelihood of growing global conflict with radical Islam is the profoundly dangerous nature of Islamic prophecy. In the same way that Christianity or Judaism have their own end-time narratives, Islam also has its vision of the last days. In fact, a poll conducted by the Pew Research Center in 2012 revealed that in many parts of the Muslim world Islamic end-time expectation is shockingly high.[3]

Islamic prophecy is so dangerous because the Islamic vision of the last days calls upon Muslims to fulfill Allah's will in an actively violent and aggressive manner. While the Bible calls Christians to turn the other cheek and to love their enemies as a witness of God's love, Islamic prophecy calls the faithful to defeat, crush, and even kill those who believe differently.

Let me give an example of how this translates into real life. One of the ministry projects that Nathan and I have been blessed to partner with has been sending doctors and medical professionals into Syria. After six years of war, the Syrian people were desperate to receive any help they could find. As such, they were quick to provide security to the teams sent in. Shortly after one of the teams arrived in the village where he would serve the Syrian people for a few months, a security guard (let's call him Mahmoud) confided in them that he was very sad. When they asked him why, he replied that he had come to really love and appreciate them, but according to Islamic teaching, when the last days arrive, as a Muslim, he is required to kill them. Obviously, this was not very comforting coming from their security guard! Ironically, the team all reported that apart from this comment, Mahmoud was a very kind and charismatic man whom they had all come to appreciate. Herein is the danger of Islamic prophecy. It encourages otherwise moderate Muslims to violence.

After the team wrestled with whether or not they should request a different security guard, they decided instead to commit to pray for Mahmoud. A few days later, the team was surprised when he came to them and asked for a Bible. They asked him why the sudden change of heart. It turned out the night before Mahmoud's wife had a dream that greatly impacted her. Jesus appeared to her and told her that she and her whole family were going to be saved. Praise the Lord for answered prayer! At the time of this writing, the story continues to unfold. Please continue to pray for Mahmoud, his family, and the entire Syrian village. While we rejoice over such testimonies, the danger of Islam remains.

Another significant reason why Islamic prophecy is so dangerous is because it influences otherwise moderate Muslims by its sense of urgency, divine empowerment, and destiny. Let's consider a few of the most basic elements of the Muslim end-time story to understand this dynamic.

First, according to Islamic teaching the last days will open with a period of wars, great chaos, suffering, and general turmoil for Muslims worldwide. In considering the many riots, protests, revolutions, civil wars, and even foreign invasions—as well as the resultant humanitarian crisis that has engulfed the Middle East over the past two decades—it is entirely understandable why so many Muslims believe they are on the very cusp of the last days. Even more specifically, Islamic tradition predicts a series of wars and battles in the region of Iraq and Syria. One much-cited prophecy speaks of an apocalyptic battle in a Syrian town called Dabiq between the Muslims and the Romans—a term interpreted to refer to the Western or Christian powers.[4]

Beginning with the American invasion of Iraq shortly after 9/11 leading up to the explosive emergence of ISIS in 2014, the reality on the ground in Iraq and Syria has created the perfect context for many Muslims to see their prophecies unfolding. In fact, Islamic prophecy and its seeming fulfillment was a very significant factor in the Islamic State's wildly successful recruiting campaign. It is one of the most significant factors in recruiting soldiers to fight for ISIS. In November 2014, the *Wall Street Journal* ran an article that analyzed the central role of Islamic prophecy in jihad recruitment. "Those ideas," it reported, "had helped attract recruits in the Middle East and beyond, said Syrian rebels who fight the group, analysts who study it, and a militant who has recently joined."[5] Will McCants, a fellow at the Brookings Institution, discussed how Islamic sacred tradition is treated by ISIS "as literal blueprints for getting in step with events leading to the imminent end of time and thus proving themselves authentic Muslims."[6] The fact that ISIS was able to draw roughly thirty thousand young people from all over the world, to leave everything behind and join the jihad in Syria and Iraq should cause all of us to shudder. Although many of the Islamic State's prophetic dreams in Iraq and Syria have been shattered for now, around the world ISIS-affiliated groups continue to expand. Islamic prophecy has impacted far more than just recruits to radical jihad. Its impact has been far more wide reaching. Throughout the few years while the

Islamic State was at its peak strength in Syria and Iraq, I would often visit online Muslim discussion groups to better understand how they were interpreting events. The degree to which the wars in Syria and Iraq were being used to cement apocalyptic expectation in the minds of many Muslims was a truly fascinating phenomenon to observe. Although different interpretations of the prophecies were common, one thing was consistent: Muslims believe Islamic prophecy is being fulfilled, and Islamic victory over the world is very close. Imagine if you will, how it would impact the Christian church globally if large numbers of believers were convinced that we were in the final stretch, truly living in the final years before Jesus returns. This is the kind of urgency and expectation that is increasingly found in many quarters of the Muslim world.

Add to the sense of urgency, triumphalism, and sense of divine destiny that accompanies so much of Islamic prophecy, and you may begin to understand the power of Muslim apocalyptic on the faithful. Consider the words of Turkish President Recep Tayyip Erdogan as he recently articulated his vision for what can rightly be called a Neo-Ottoman Empire: "It is the Turkish nation's destiny to shoulder the burden of this entire geography from the Balkans to the Caucasia and the Central Africa to the Central Asia. Geography is destiny and we will not escape our destiny."[7]

The belief that one is fulfilling divine destiny has always been a powerful tool used to gain the hearts of the faithful. In 1453, when Mehmet Fetih was preparing his soldiers to conquer the Christian city of Constantinople, it is said that he sent Muslim preachers into the camps of his soldiers at night to expound an ancient prophecy ascribed to Muhammad: "Verily you shall conquer Constantinople. What a wonderful leader will her leader be, and what a wonderful army will that army be!"[8] They were the proud prophesied ones, the chosen, who would follow Mehmet into battle, finally bringing to completion the words of their beloved prophet. As it was in the fifteenth century among the Turkish soldiers, so also today there is a growing sense among many Muslims globally that the divine winds of destiny are blowing afresh.

Whether it is among the tens of thousands of recruits to ISIS or the foot-soldiers of the emerging Turkish regional ascendancy, Islamic end-time prophecy is a powerful drug that must not be underestimated. Perhaps this is one of the reasons why Jesus so emphasized the danger of deception in the last days.

No doubt, the days ahead will be greatly defined by the multitudes who are deceived by Islamic end-time prophecies. In fact, it may very well be through the vast collection of counterfeit Muslim prophecies that Satan has long prepared a large segment of the world to follow the Antichrist as if he were their awaited savior. Understanding what Islam teaches regarding the Mahdi may give us great insight into Satan's grand plan of resistance in the days ahead.

ANTICHRIST: ISLAM'S AWAITED MESSIAH?

This leads us to the final, and perhaps most significant, reason why Islamic prophecy is so dangerous. In many other striking ways, Islamic prophecy functions as a mirror image to biblical prophecy, with great potential to mislead Muslims into essentially *supporting the wrong team*, and actually giving their allegiance to the Antichrist. Let me explain.

After the prophesied period of great suffering for Muslims, Islamic prophecy expects the emergence of an Islamic messiah-figure known as the Mahdi. Ibn Kathir, the renowned fourteenth-century Muslim scholar introduces his readers to the Mahdi thusly:

> After the lesser signs of the Hour appear and increase, mankind will have reached a stage of great suffering. Then the awaited Mahdi will appear; He is the first of the greater clear signs of the Hour.[9]

According to Islamic prophecy, the Mahdi will unite the Muslim world under his leadership. According to this prophetic tradition, the Mahdi "will pave the way for and establish the government of the religion of Muhammad. . . . Every believer will be obligated to support him.[10] Not only is the awaited Mahdi believed to bring deliverance and unity to the Muslim world, but even more important, he is believed to lead a series of military victories over non-Muslims. According to Muslim author Sideeque M. A. Veliankode: "The Mahdi will establish right and justice in the world and eliminate evil and corruption. He will fight against the enemies of the Muslims who would be victorious."[11] As Ayatollah Baqir al-Sadr and Ayatullah Murtada Mutahhari said:

> He will reappear on the appointed day, and then he will fight against the forces of evil, lead a world revolution, and set up a new world order based on justice, righteousness, and virtue... ultimately the righteous will take the world administration in their hands and Islam will be victorious over all the religions.[12]

Egyptian authors Muhammad ibn Izzat, Muhammad 'Arif, describe the Mahdi's last days military victories thusly:

> He is the precursor of the victory of the Truth and the fall of all tyrants. He heralds the end of injustice and oppression and the beginning of the final rising of the sun of Islam which will never again set and which will ensure happiness and the elevation of mankind. . . . The Mahdi is one of Allah's clear signs which will soon be made evident to everyone.[13]

Numerous Islamic traditions picture the non-Muslim world coming to Islam as a result of the Mahdi's conquests. Abduallrahman Kelani, author of, *The Last Apocalypse*, describes the many battles of the Mahdi:

> [A]l-Mahdi will receive a pledge of allegiance as a caliph for Muslims. He will lead Muslims in many battles of jihad. His reign will be a caliphate that follows the guidance of the Prophet. Many battles will ensue between Muslims and the disbelievers during the Mahdi's reign.[14]

Even Adnan Oktar, a moderate Turkish cleric and author, refers to the Mahdi's invasion of numerous non-Muslim lands when he predicts that "the Mahdi will invade all the places between East and West."[15] Other Muslim prophecies specifically speak of the defeat of "the Romans" as well the Jews, or the State of Israel.

In my book *Islamic Antichrist*, I work through several other elements of the Islamic narrative to show that Muslim expectation concerning the Mahdi aligns rather seamlessly with the biblical descriptions of the Antichrist and his particular goals in the last days. For example, Islamic prophecy says the Mahdi will rule for a period of seven years. The prophet Daniel informs us that the Antichrist will enter into a covenant with Israel, specifically for a seven-year period before Jesus returns. Islamic prophecy portrays the Mahdi as establishing his seat of global Islamic authority specifically on the Temple Mount in Jerusalem. Some passages in the Bible state that the Antichrist will set himself up on the Temple Mount, demanding the complete obedience of all people (see 2 Thess. 2:4). Various traditions and Islamic scholars describe the focus of his military and ideological campaigns as being directed toward Jews and Christians above all other people groups. According to the Bible, this will also be the Antichrist's primary target for conquest (see Rev. 12-13).

We must be clear here that Muslim prophecies are in no way divinely inspired. In no way should this counterfeit prophetic tradition be equated with biblical prophecies. The point in examining these things is simply to gain a glimpse into what very much appears to be the very playbook, as it were, of the enemy. In fact, it is not at all unreasonable to believe that through Islamic end-time prophecies, the devil has prepared much of the Muslim world to receive the Antichrist as if he is their long-awaited Messiah.

Even if we are considering Muslim apocalyptic hopes from a completely secular perspective, the widespread expectation throughout much of the Muslim world in a coming messianic figure is extremely troubling. Historically, several individuals have arisen and claimed to be the awaited Mahdi, each time gathering large followings, and nearly always leading to a bloody confrontation.[16] These historical Mahdi movements however, have always been fairly localized and limited. Today, with globalization, social connectivity, and the ease of communication, the potential for a messiah figure to quickly gain a global following is a very real possibility. Knowing that the Bible says a large segment of the world will follow the Antichrist, we may reasonably infer that it will be specifically through Islamic prophetic expectation that Satan will accomplish his final great deception.

IT'S BIBLICAL

Perhaps the most important reason why we are right to expect the future to be defined by militant Islam is simply because the Bible essentially states that this will be the case. First, the Bible makes it clear that in the last days the Antichrist—a satanically empowered dictator—will gather together a multinational coalition that will invade Israel and conquer Jerusalem (cf. Joel 3; Zech. 12, 14; Ez. 38-39; Rev. 11:2).

How does this prove that the Antichrist and his armies will largely be Muslim? The answer lies in simply identifying where he and his primary followers all come from. To answer that question, we must first identify the primary context of the last-days biblical narrative. What is the primary geographic focus of the Bible's prophecies concerning the last days. The answer to this question is very simple.

IT'S ALL ABOUT ISRAEL

Anyone who wishes to properly understand the biblical narrative, absolutely must grasp a very basic point. Geographically speaking, the story of the Bible is thoroughly centered around Israel and Jerusalem. The culmination of the story in the last days, revolves around this specific piece of land and city. Jerusalem is the location where Jesus will return to reestablish the throne of his forefather David. As the angel Gabriel explained to young Mary:

> And behold, you will conceive in your womb and bear a son, and you shall name Him Jesus. He will be great and will be called the Son of the Most High; and *the Lord God will give Him the throne of His father David*; and He will reign over the house of Jacob forever, and His kingdom will have no end. (Luke 1:31-33)

It is specifically from Mount Zion in Jerusalem that Jesus will rule the nations (Ps. 2:6). With that said, what do we find when we look at the biblical descriptions of the coming Antichrist empire?

THE SURROUNDING NATIONS

Repeatedly, the Scriptures state that it will be "the surrounding" nations or peoples that will comprise the coming Antichrist empire and take the lead in invading Israel. Let's consider just a few examples.

Speaking of the armies of the Antichrist, the prophet Joel said, "Hasten and come, *all you surrounding nations*, and gather yourselves there . . . for there I will sit to judge *all the surrounding nations*" (Joel 3:11–12, emphasis added). In Zechariah, the Lord speaks similarly: "Behold, I am going to make Jerusalem a cup that causes reeling to *all the peoples around*; and when the siege is against Jerusalem, it will also be against Judah. . . . In that day I will make the clans of Judah like a firepot among pieces of wood and a flaming torch among sheaves, so they will consume on the right hand and on the left *all the surrounding peoples*, while the inhabitants of Jerusalem again dwell on their own sites in Jerusalem. "(Zech. 12:2, 6, emphasis added).

Ezekiel also spoke of the day when the people of Israel will no longer be surrounded by people who despise them: "And for the house of Israel there shall be no more a brier to prick or a thorn to hurt them among *all their neighbors* who have treated them with contempt. Then they will know that I am the Lord GOD" (Ezekiel 28:24, ESV, emphasis added). The phrase translated here as "all their neighbors" is the same word used in both Joel and Zechariah. It is the Hebrew word, *cayviv,* which refers to those nations which are around Israel, her neighbors. Obviously, Israel's neighbors are the many Muslim majority nations of the Middle East and North Africa.

THE NATIONS OF THE ANTICHRIST

This simple, yet critical point cannot be emphasized enough. Throughout the Scriptures, whenever the nations of the Antichrist are mentioned they are *all* Middle Eastern and North Africa nations. Every single time the Bible mentions, lists, or names the nations, peoples, tribes, or groups that will attack Israel in the last days, they are always—down to the very last name—all Muslim majority nations. Conversely, there is not a single mention by name of a European, or non-Muslim majority nation being judged in the day of the Lord for attacking Israel. The Bible overwhelmingly, repeatedly, and consistently lists Muslim majority nations as the primary players in the coming last-days empire of the Antichrist, that will wreak havoc across much of the world.

Let's zero in on some even more specific passages.

THE NATIONS OF ANTICHRIST IN EZEKIEL

In Ezekiel 25 we find a very clear prophecy that speaks of the Lord's divine judgment directed against Ammon, Moab, and Edom because of how they treated "the house of Judah." Again, these three kingdoms inhabited what is modern day Jordan. The prophet says that by executing undue "vengeance" against His chosen people, He Himself is "greatly offended." For this reason, the Lord will judge them with "wrathful rebukes."

But the text speaks of much more than just Ammon, Moab, and Edom. It also mentions Dedan, which is a city located in what is now central Saudi Arabia, known in modern times as *Al-`Ula*. The prophecy also goes on to mention the Philistines and the Cherethites, pointing to regions that are today associated with the Gaza strip. A few chapters later in Ezekiel 30, many other nations are marked for judgment at the day of the Lord:

> The word of the LORD came to me saying, "Son of man, prophesy, and say, Thus says the Lord GOD: "Wail, 'Alas for the day!' *For the day is near, the day of the LORD is near;* it will be a day of clouds, a time of doom for the nations. A sword shall come upon Egypt, and anguish shall be in Ethiopia, when the slain fall in Egypt, and her wealth is carried away, and her foundations are torn down. Ethiopia, Put, Lud, and all Arabia, Libya, and the people of the land that is in league, shall fall with them by the sword." (Ezekiel 30:1–5, emphasis added)

The ultimate context of the passage is the day of the Lord, and Christ's return. And here, as in so many other passages, the Messiah comes to execute judgment against the enemies of His people, Israel. Included in the list of those marked for judgment are Egypt, Cush (Sudan), Put (North Africa), Lud (Turkey), Arabia, and Libya.

THE NATIONS OF ANTICHRIST IN ZEPHANIAH

Following in the footsteps of all the other prophets, Zephaniah prophesied that on "the day of the LORD's anger" (Zeph. 2:3, NKJV) Gaza, Ashkelon, Ashdod, Ekron, the Cherethites, Canaan, and the land of the Philistines will all be utterly ruined. Together, these names point us to the whole region around the Gaza Strip. But beyond judgment against Gaza, the prophecy continues with a warning concerning the future of Moab, Ammon, Cush (Sudan), as well as Assyria and Nineveh:

> "I have heard the taunts of Moab and the revilings of the Ammonites, how they have taunted my people and made boasts against their territory. Therefore, as I live," declares the LORD of hosts, the God of Israel, "Moab shall become like Sodom, and the Ammonites like Gomorrah, a land possessed by nettles and salt pits, and a waste forever. The remnant of my people shall plunder them, and the survivors of my nation shall possess them. . . . You also, O Cushites [Sudan], shall be slain by my sword. And he will stretch out his hand against the north and destroy Assyria [Syria, Turkey, Lebanon, and Iraq], and he will make Nineveh a desolation, a dry waste like the desert. (Zephaniah 2:8–9, 12–13, ESV)

During Zephaniah's day, Assyria straddled the borders of modern-day Turkey, Syria, Lebanon, and Iraq. Of course, it all goes without saying that all of these nations and regions are dominated by Islam. Because the Scriptures repeatedly emphasize Muslim majority nations as being singled out for judgment and defeat at the day of the Lord, then it is only reasonable to conclude that this is the part of the world from which the Antichrist and his coalition will arise.

TREADING THE WINE-PRESS

Finally we come to the book of Revelation. It is in chapter 19 that we find arguably the most well-known passage concerning Christ's return in the entire Bible. In dramatic imagery, Jesus bursts forth from heaven with eyes of fire, riding upon a white horse with "the armies of heaven" following him:

> Then I saw heaven opened, and behold, a white horse! The one sitting on it is called Faithful and True, and in righteousness he judges and makes war. His eyes are like a flame of fire, and on his head are many diadems; and he has a name written that no one knows but himself. He is clothed in a robe dipped in blood, and His name is called The Word of God. And the armies which are in heaven, clothed in fine linen, white and clean, were following Him on white horses. From His mouth comes a sharp sword, so that with it He may strike down the nations, and He will rule them with a rod of iron; And He treads the winepress of the fury of the wrath of God the Almighty. And on his robe and on His thigh He has a name written, "KING OF KINGS AND LORD OF LORDS." (vv. 11–16)

Most Christians are familiar with this passage. Yet few are aware whose blood is soaking Jesus' robes. Many think it is Jesus' own blood or the blood of the martyrs. But the real answer is found in Isaiah. Let's look at the passage:

> Who is this who comes from Edom, in crimsoned garments from Bozrah, he who is splendid in his apparel, marching in the greatness of his strength? "It is I, speaking in righteousness, mighty to save." Why is your apparel red, and your garments like his who treads in the winepress? "I have trodden the winepress alone, and from the peoples no one was with me; I trod them in my anger and trampled them in my wrath; their lifeblood spattered on my garments, and stained all my apparel. For the day of vengeance was in my heart, and my year of redemption had come." (Isaiah 63:1–4, ESV)

In this dramatic passage, Isaiah the prophet is looking eastward from Jerusalem. He sees a majestic and determined figure—Jesus the Messiah—marching victoriously toward His throne in Jerusalem. Jesus is marching out from Bozrah, which was the capital city of ancient Edom. It is very close to Petra, in modern day Jordan. Few are aware that it is in this passage that we get the concept of Jesus treading "the winepress of the fury of the wrath of God the Almighty." For here, Isaiah informs us that Jesus, the victorious warrior—the Lion of the tribe of Judah—will actually crush the enemies of God like grapes, soaking his robes with their blood.

As the Lord warned the serpent so long ago, when the seed of the woman, the promised Messiah, came it would mean the end of Satan and his followers: "He shall bruise you on the head, and you shall bruise him on the heel" (Gen. 3:15). Though Satan has struck the heels of God's people throughout history, when Jesus returns, He will not only crush Satan, but Satan's followers as well. He will tread the winepress of the wrath of God Almighty. But we must also not miss the fact that it will specifically be in Edom that God's enemies will be crushed. When Jesus returns, the Bible describes Him destroying His enemies, specifically in what is today southern Jordan and northwest Saudi Arabia.

Throughout the Bible we have seen repeatedly and abundantly that whenever specific nations are named and highlighted for the judgment of God when Jesus returns, it is always regions or nations that are today vastly dominated by Islam. This is the part of the world that the Bible is screaming at us to look to. This is going to be the hot spot, not only for the activity of Satan in the last days but also for the Lord and the advance of His eternal Gospel.

In the last two chapters we've looked at several distinct reasons why we should expect radical Islam to fulfill the Bible's descriptions concerning the system of the Antichrist and his empire, thus producing the final and greatest catastrophe.

First, we looked at Muslim demographics. As much of the Western world continues to witness a decline in both birthrates and church attendance, Islam continues to experience steady growth forward. The future belongs to those who show up for it, and right now, Islam appears to be the future. Barring a drastic demographic shift, Islam will continue to play a profound role in defining our collective future. Even today, Islam is the single greatest source of Christian persecution globally. To see the system of the Antichrist as something other than Islam requires that we see an entirely new religious system being embraced throughout the world. While anything is most certainly possible, the reality is that things like this normally take decades, if not generations. The likelihood of an entirely new religious system sweeping the world in the next few decades seems highly unlikely.

Second, we examined the fact that Islam is a fundamentally violent and intolerant religious system. Anyone who honestly examines the Qur'an, the life of Muhammad, or the example left behind by Islam's earliest founders, will be faced with the undeniable reality that Islam was founded upon and calls for violence and conflict with non-Muslims. While the majority of Muslims are most certainly not militants or terrorists, there is indeed a significant enough percentage of Muslims who do study Islamic sacred documents and history and seek to implement what they read that it would be rather *unreasonable* if we did not expect them to sow seeds of intolerance that lead to violence and produce a bitter harvest for the world.

This expectation is particularly reasonable in light of the third reality we examined: the exploding popularity of violent jihadist ideology. Not only have ISIS and other radical groups been wildly successful in recruiting an astounding number of willing volunteers to join their causes, but they have also been tremendously successful in using social media and videos to their advantage. Among large segments of the burgeoning Muslim youth population throughout the world, jihad is increasingly fashionable. Instead of seeing moderate reform movements within Islam, we see radical groups growing in popularity. This current trend is a horrible portent for what we may expect to see in the years and decades ahead.

The fourth issue that we discussed is the blowback that the Muslim martyrdom culture creates. What this simply means is that the more we attempt to use military might to extinguish violent jihadis, the more they tend to multiply. Because Islam has such a vibrant culture of martyrdom, the more jihadis who are killed, the more heroes and legends are created. It is a perpetual lose-lose scenario. Meanwhile, the larger jihadi movement is able to bleed even the most well-resourced military of its resources and soldiers, all the while expanding their global networks. Because this war is ultimately spiritual, it will never be fully resolved until Jesus returns.

The fifth reason why Islam will continue to emerge as the final great challenge to the people of God is because of the many profound ways in which Islamic theology, practice, and goals all perfectly align with the biblical descriptions of the coming Antichrist system. In other words, because Islam already matches the primary biblical descriptions concerning the last-days system of the Antichrist, we have no reason to look elsewhere. It is quite likely that we are already looking at that which the prophets foresaw.

Further, we examined the dangerous nature of Islamic prophecy. Beyond the many ways in which foundational Islamic theology aligns perfectly with the biblical descriptions of the system of the Antichrist, in a far more profound way, Islam's end-time prophecies seem to be tailor-made to deceive the Muslim world specifically into following the Antichrist, as though he were their long awaited and prophesied leader.

The last reason that we examined as to why we are right to expect the future to be defined by militant Islam is simply because the Bible essentially says so. We discussed the fact that the Bible is thoroughly Israel-centric. The primary geographic context of the great wars of the last days revolve and center around Jerusalem. This being the case, we then looked at several passages that specifically refer to the invading armies of the Antichrist as "the surrounding nations," or "neighbors," of Israel. We then explored the fact that through the prophets, the Bible repeatedly names the nations that will follow the Antichrist. They are all Middle Eastern and North African Islamic nations. Biblical geography points us to the nations that surround Israel, which is the very heartland of Islam. Again, unless an entirely new religion comes to sweep throughout the Middle East, which is extremely unlikely to happen in our lifetimes, we simply have no reason to look to anything else other than Islam.

Of course, there are several other issues that we could discuss in more detail, such as the growing movement to revive the Caliphate (Islamic government) over all of the Muslim world. We could discuss the degree to which hatred of the Jewish people has become an epidemic throughout the Muslim world. In these matters we find yet more perfect parallels to the biblical descriptions concerning the goals and the mission of the Antichrist and his hordes.

All things considered, when we insert the key of Islam into the often-confusing puzzle of biblical prophecy, *it fits*. The previously hazy contours of the social, religious, and geopolitical landscape as described by the biblical prophets are coming into near perfect alignment with what we are presently witnessing in our day. To see Islam as the last great challenge to the church simply makes sense. What is now unfolding throughout the earth, with the spread of radical Islam, terrorism, and the focus of the world being turned back to the Middle East is indeed that which the biblical prophets spoke of. So once more, let us restate, until Jesus returns, Islam will continue to be the single greatest external challenge to the church and God's people throughout the world. The profound deception inherent within Islam, particularly it's end-time prophetic traditions, will lead to the greatest man-made global disaster that mankind has ever faced. Jesus called this time the "great tribulation, such as has not occurred since the beginning of the world until now, nor ever will" (Matt. 24:21). Surely, we who are serious about heeding the words of Jesus and recognizing the handwriting on the wall will take these things to heart and soberly consider how we are to respond. This will be the subject of chapter 10. Before we discuss that, however, we must pause to discuss how all of this fits within the Lord's ultimate sovereign plans for the end times. It is a reality that very few of us like to discuss, but which is absolutely necessary.

Today I walked with the refugees along a path toward the Serbian border. It put the situation into full context for me. After being unloaded from the train, the refugees would begin walking the two kilometers to the border, mostly in groups. I, along with the guys who were with me, would walk with a group to a certain point then turn back and do the same with another group of refugees. As I walked with each cluster, I would move to the center so I was surrounded by everyone. Though it was only momentary, I wanted to walk in their shoes as one of them. Nearly every time, I would find someone who knew English. Generally I would ask the same questions: "Where are you from?" "Where are you going?" "Why did you leave your country?" The stories were similar: "We are from Syria or Afghanistan." "We are going to Germany or Holland." "We fled because of ISIS or the Taliban."

—SYRIAN REFUGEE CRISIS, PERSONAL JOURNAL, OCTOBER 10, 2015

9

THE LORD'S PURPOSE FOR THE ANTICHRIST

Do not fear what you are about to suffer.

—REVELATION 2:10, NIV

ONLY HOURS BEFORE Jesus would be betrayed, mutilated, and hung between heaven and earth, He passed on to His disciples one of the most critical lessons He would ever teach. Jesus knew that His suffering and death would result in tremendous disillusionment and pain among His disciples. The one who they believed to be the long-awaited Messiah was about to die a humiliating death fit for a rank criminal. For most of them the next few days would entail the greatest trial they had ever faced up until that point. Understanding this Jesus instructed them:

> I am the true vine, and My Father is the vinedresser. Every branch in Me that does not bear fruit, He takes away; and every branch that bears fruit, He prunes it so that it may bear more fruit. You are already clean because of the word which I have spoken to you. Abide in Me, and I

in you. As the branch cannot bear fruit of itself unless it abides in the vine, so neither can you unless you abide in Me. I am the vine, you are the branches; he who abides in Me and I in him, he bears much fruit, for apart from Me you can do nothing. If anyone does not abide in Me, he is thrown away as a branch and dries up; and they gather them, and cast them into the fire and they are burned. (John 15:1-6)

What exactly was Jesus's point? The longer I walk with Christ, the more I am convinced that in every tragedy, through every wave or season of suffering we face, the Lord is seeking to beat a very simple truth into our hearts: He is the sole source of life; apart from Him, we have absolutely nothing and can do absolutely nothing of any lasting and eternal value. Every time we encounter some kind of pain, we are faced with the choice to either rely on our own strength—*as if a mere branch has any actual life in itself*—or to recognize our own fundamental dependence on Him. This is the very goal of Christian maturity, to humbly lean fully into Jesus, the only source of life, hope, or strength. The spiritually mature do not trust in their own abilities or sufficiency. Instead they are filled with a complete trust and reliance upon Jesus.

Beyond all of the complex mysteries of this life, this is the "purpose" if you will, of pain. Difficulties, tragedies, suffering are all opportunities for growth. Even as Jesus Himself demonstrated perfect obedience to God "from the things which He suffered" (Heb. 5:8), so also the Lord has chosen to use these things to help bring us toward the place of spiritual maturity. This basic truth, as difficult as it is to accept, is a theme found throughout the Scriptures. Of course such lessons never come easy. No one who experiences any kind of pain has a natural appreciation for it. Yet, the Lord tenderly appeals to us to avoid interpreting pain in a purely negative manner: "My son, do not despise the LORD's discipline, and do not resent his rebuke" (Pro. 3:11, ESV). Instead, we are to view the pains of this life as actual evidence of His parental affections and delight over us because "for whom the LORD loves He reproves, even as a father corrects the son in whom he delights" (v. 12). Instead of viewing pain as evidence of God's disapproval, the Lord says that he actually brings these things onto those He loves, as an opportunity for growth. In the book of Revelation, Jesus reminds us of this critical truth: "Those whom I love I reprove and discipline" (3:19). And yet once more, in the book of Hebrews we read that if there is a total lack of pain in our lives, then we should be concerned:

> Endure hardship as discipline; God is treating you as his children. For what children are not disciplined by their father? If you are not disciplined—and everyone undergoes discipline—then you are not legitimate, not true sons and daughters at all. Moreover, we have all had human fathers who disciplined us and we respected them for it. How much more should we submit to the Father of spirits and live! They disciplined us for a little while as they thought best; but God disciplines us for our good, in order that we may share in his holiness. No discipline seems pleasant at the time, but painful. Later on, however, it produces a harvest of righteousness and peace for those who have been trained by it. Therefore, strengthen your feeble arms and weak knees. "Make level paths for your feet," so that the lame may not be disabled, but rather healed. (Hebrews 12:7-13, NIV)

Most of us misinterpret painful circumstances that enter our lives as God's disapproval of, or even anger toward, us. Although this is a very natural reaction, it is a tragic error that we must learn to avoid. Christians must learn to interpret personal pain as God's loving, parental offer to grow closer to Him. Those who suffer are actually considered "blessed" and exhorted not to "despise the discipline of the Almighty. For he wounds, but he also binds up; he injures, but his hands also heal" (Job 5:17-18, NIV).

James, the brother of Jesus even goes so far as to exhort us to interpret various trials joyously, seeing them as opportunities for spiritual development unto perfection:

Count it all joy, my brethren, when you fall into various trials, knowing that the testing of your faith produces endurance. But let endurance have its perfect result, that you may be perfect and complete, lacking in nothing. (James 1:2–4)

Finally, in like manner, the apostle Peter also encourages us to so see the redemptive potential of suffering as having a purifying purpose, that we would actually rejoice when we are faced with trials:

In this you greatly rejoice, though now for a little while, if need be, you have been grieved by various trials, so that the proof of your faith, being much more precious than gold which is perishable, even though tested by fire, may be found to result in praise and glory and honor at the revelation of Jesus Christ; and though you do not see Him now, but believe in Him, you rejoice with joy inexpressible and full of glory, obtaining as the outcome of your faith, the salvation of your souls. (1 Peter 1:6–9)

TO BECOME A PEOPLE OF PRAYER

So while it is clear that the more general, broader purpose of suffering in this age is to provide us with an opportunity to become a people more mature, more dependent on Jesus, in an even more specific sense, it is to make us into a people of prayer. Surely there is no better gauge of one's reliance on God than their prayer life. The degree to which someone does not pray is the degree to which they have chosen to rely on themselves and their own strength. Those who are reliant on the Lord will quite naturally pray more. Those who rely on themselves will pray less. It's very simple. If a season of pain does not result in us praying more, then in essence we have failed that particular test. Whether or not we maintained our dignity during trials is not what determines if we passed. Instead, it is determined by whether or not we cried out to the Lord and grew in our reliance on Him and in prayer. This is why Jesus finishes His lesson of the vine and branches with an amazing promise. If we cooperate with the Lord's work of pruning our hearts and lives, if we become a person more dependent on Him, then we will receive far greater authority in prayer:

> If you abide in Me, and My words abide in you, you will ask what you desire, and it shall be done for you. By this My Father is glorified, that you bear much fruit; so you will be my disciples. (John 15:7–8, NIV)

What a wonderful promise! What Christian does not want to walk in greater authority in prayer, to see our prayers answered more regularly? The key is found in learning the lessons of the parable of the vine and the branches.

TO RECLAIM A THEOLOGY OF SUFFERING

Why then, is suffering a topic that is rarely preached in most churches today? Why is it that such a basic building block of the Christian life is rarely elaborated upon in pulpits across most of the world? Undeniably, the modern church, particularly the Western church, has a profoundly underdeveloped theology of suffering. We have lost the apostolic teaching concerning suffering, persecution, and even martyrdom that fueled the early Christian movement. Today, in far too many theological circles, an overly realized eschatology has frequently misled many to believe that all of the promises of the age to come belong to them fully now. They have lost the pattern of suffering before glory that Jesus so clearly demonstrated—"Did not the Messiah have to suffer these things and then enter his glory?" (Luke 24:26, NIV)—and to which we are likewise called to imitate: "To this you were called, because Christ suffered for you, leaving you an example, that you should follow in his steps." (1 Pet. 2:21, NIV). I recently read excerpts from a popular Christian book that claims, apart from persecution, obedient Christians are entirely exempt from any form of suffering in this age. The degree to which such unbiblical claims are increasingly being taught and embraced in certain quarters of the church is actually terrifying. If the people of God throughout the world are soon to face the greatest time of tribulation they have ever faced, then it is absolutely imperative that we gather around this topic more frequently, reminding ourselves afresh of the truth concerning the Lord's ultimate and good purpose for pain and suffering. In the same way that the disciples who were about to face such a great trial needed the lesson of the vine and the branches, so also do we, as the last days church need to learn the lessons taught in this parable as we approach the final great trial.

GOD'S PURPOSE FOR ANTICHRIST

If we are unable to understand the redemptive purpose of suffering, then we most certainly will never accept the fact that the Lord Himself will allow the Antichrist to rise to power, bringing about the worst tribulation in human history. If we are able to grasp the redemptive potential of pain, however, then we will likewise be able to grasp the Lord's purposes in sovereignly allowing the last great dictator to arise. Even as the Lord has always used pain to break people of their pride and self-reliance and bring them to a place of greater maturity, so also will He use the painful crescendo of human history to offer all people one final opportunity to forsake their pride and draw closer to Him. While the coming time of trial will impact everyone globally, there are three specific groups who will benefit most from the opportunities, if you will, afforded by the coming tribulation. The three primary groups are: Christians or Messianic believers, Israel, and the larger unbelieving world. Let's consider each group in turn.

TO BRING THE SAINTS TO MATURITY

Christians are exhorted throughout the Scriptures to view suffering, pain, or difficulties as an opportunity to grow in spiritual maturity. This theme continues in many passages specific to the last days. In the book of Revelation 19 a great multitude in heaven erupts into a thunderous chorus shouting "Hallelujah! For the Lord our God, the Almighty, reigns" (v. 6). The reason for all of the celebration is twofold: first, "the marriage of the Lamb has come" and second, because "His bride has made herself ready" (v. 7). There is no question that the church throughout history has accomplished many beautiful, marvelous, and heroic things, but it also has participated in an endless array of divisions, compromises, scandals, and even outright atrocities. Yet despite her often-shameful track record, the Scriptures tell us that in the last days, the bride of Christ will attain a degree of purity not known before so that she will be ready for the Lord. The church will indeed "clothe herself in fine linen, bright and clean; for the fine linen is the righteous acts of the saints" (v. 8).

This picture of the purity of the saints in the last days is surprisingly found in a book of the Bible most don't associate with prophecy. Although most Christians think of the Song of Solomon as being purely about romantic or sexual love between a husband and wife, many of the hundreds of commentaries written throughout the centuries on this book speak to a deeper spiritual interpretation, one that relates to either the corporate people of God or even the individual Christian and Jesus, "the beloved." With this view in mind, there is perhaps no passage in the Bible that more beautifully and poetically depicts the saints of the end times than Song of Songs 8:5. We see the bride of Christ emerging from the wilderness of this tribulation-filled age, fully dependent on the Lord: "Who is this, coming up out of the wilderness, leaning on her beloved?" (Song of Songs 8:5).

This then is the purpose of the great tribulation for Christians who are alive during this final period of history. The Lord will use the coming difficulties to purify the saints from entanglement with this world, so that they will emerge from the trials of the wilderness fully leaning on their Beloved: *Jesus, the Bridegroom.*

TO BRING ISRAEL TO MATURITY

The next group who will be transformed through the final trial is Israel. One of the greatest results of the great tribulation will be all of Israel coming into complete and permanent covenantal faithfulness to the Lord. That God will discipline His people, resulting in their turning to Him forever, is a theme taught throughout the Bible. As far back as the days of Israel's wilderness wanderings, through the Song of Moses, the

Lord spoke of the last days when He would discipline them with great "calamity." Then, "When He sees that their strength is gone, and there is none remaining, bond or free" (Deut. 32:36), He will reveal Himself to them as the only true God above all other gods. He will declare to them: "See now that I, I am He, and there is no god besides Me; It is I who put to death and give life. I have wounded and it is I who heal, and there is no one who can deliver from My hand (Deut. 32:39).

Jeremiah spoke of the time when God would "restore the fortunes of My people Israel and Judah" and "bring them back to the land that I gave to their forefathers and they shall possess it." (Jer. 30:1-2). Before they are able to take perpetual possession of the land, however, Jeremiah speaks of a terrible time of tribulation: "For thus says the LORD, 'I have heard a sound of terror, of dread, and there is no peace" (v. 5). He then asks the question as to whether or not a man can give birth to a baby. It is a rhetorical question, of course, of which the answer is a resounding *no*. If this is the case, then "Why do I see every man with his hands on his loins, as a woman in childbirth? And why have all faces turned pale?" (v. 6). The people of the land of Israel are portrayed as being gripped by agony and fear. He concludes: "Alas! for that day is great, there is none like it; and it is the time of Jacob's distress, but he will be saved from it" (v. 7).

Nearly a century later, the prophet Daniel also spoke of this time: "And there will be a time of distress such as never occurred since there was a nation until that time. . . . As soon as they finish shattering the power of the holy people, all these events will be completed" (Dan. 12:1, 7).

Finally, Jesus Himself, expanding on all that had been prophesied before Him said this concerning Jerusalem and the whole region of Judah or southern Israel: "For then there will be a great tribulation, such as has not occurred since the beginning of the world until now, nor ever will. Unless those days had been cut short, no life would have been saved; but for the sake of the elect those days will be cut short" (Matt. 24:21-22). And from Luke's account of the same sermon we read:

But when you see Jerusalem surrounded by armies, then recognize that her desolation is near. Then those who are in Judea must flee to the mountains, and those who are in the midst of the city must leave, and those who are in the country must not enter the city; because these are days of vengeance, so that all things which are written will be fulfilled. Woe to those who are pregnant and to those who are nursing babies in those days; for there will be great distress upon the land and wrath to this people; and they will fall by the edge of the sword, and will be led captive into all the nations; and Jerusalem will be trampled under foot by the Gentiles until the times of the Gentiles are fulfilled. (Luke 21:20-24)

For those of us who love Israel and genuinely yearn to see their national salvation, these future realities are very painful. It is essential that we do not read of these things in an emotionally detached manner but instead allow ourselves to be gripped with the weight of what the Scriptures teach here. It is also essential that we do not lose sight of the end result of this time of unparalleled calamity. After Israel is "shattered" and brought to "the end of their strength," then they will finally come to the place of humility and brokenness, and they will all together turn to the Lord in utter dependence and faithfulness. The Bible is replete with allusions to Jacob's trouble, or the great tribulation, and it also is filled with prophecies concerning Jacob's salvation and fullness. Perhaps the most referenced passage about Jacob's salvation is found in Zechariah, who speaks of the Lord pouring out on "the house of David and the inhabitants of Jerusalem, the Spirit of grace" (Zech. 12:10). But the Lord also spoke through Ezekiel the prophet of the glorious day when, "the house of Israel will know that I am the LORD their God from that day onward. . . . I will not hide My face from them any longer, for I will have poured out My Spirit on the house of Israel" (Ezek. 39:22, 29 cf., 36:22–28). Through Isaiah God also speaks of the glorious days for Israel when, "'My Spirit which is upon you, and My words which I have put in your mouth shall not depart from your mouth, nor from the mouth of your offspring, nor from the mouth of your offspring's offspring,' says the Lord, 'from now and forever'" (Isa. 59:21). And yet again, through Jeremiah, the Lord spoke of the day when he "will forgive their iniquity" and remember their sin "no more" (Jeremiah 31:34). This is exactly what the apostle Paul referred to when he jubilantly spoke of the appointed day when "all Israel will be saved" (Rom. 11:26).

The Lord will indeed bring Israel to the end of its self-reliance. For all of their vigilance, determination, and military prowess, the Lord will teach His people that He alone is the source of their salvation. Like those young Jewish disciples that walked with Jesus so long ago, modern Israel will come to the knowledge that they also are mere branches. Jesus alone is the vine and the only source of all life. The Lord has chosen to use the Antichrist to bring about a time of unparalleled catastrophe, to bring Israel to salvation. It is absolutely imperative that discerning believers recognize this biblical truth and begin preparing even now, practically and emotionally, how to rightly respond during this critical moment of redemptive history.

TO GIVE UNBELIEVERS THE OPPORTUNITY TO REPENT

The final group that will benefit from the catastrophes of the Last Days are unbelievers. The Bible emphasizes it will be a final opportunity for them to repent. It is for this reason, that Paul exhorts believers to embrace the judgments or disciplines of God, not merely as opportunities to draw closer to God but also to escape the ultimate condemnation that unbelievers will face on the day of judgment:

> Nevertheless, when we are judged in this way by the Lord, we are being disciplined so that we will not be finally condemned with the world. (1 Corinthians 11:32, NIV)

In Revelation 9 we discover that the purpose of the disastrous plagues of the last days is specifically to give men the opportunity to repent:

The rest of mankind, who were not killed by these plagues, did not repent of the works of their hands, so as not to worship demons, and the idols of gold and of silver and of brass and of stone and of wood, which can neither see nor hear nor walk; and they did not repent of their murders nor of their sorceries nor of their immorality nor of their thefts. (Revelation 9:20-21)

In Revelation 16 we see that the reaction of mankind toward the "natural disasters" that the Lord will bring upon the earth is not to repent but to harden themselves and blaspheme God:

Men were scorched with fierce heat; and they blasphemed the name of God who has the power over these plagues, and they did not repent so as to give Him glory. Then the fifth angel poured out his bowl on the throne of the beast, and his kingdom became darkened; and they gnawed their tongues because of pain, and they blasphemed the God of heaven because of their pains and their sores; and they did not repent of their deeds. (Revelation 16:9-11)

Despite the pains brought about by God's judgments, as a whole, unbelievers do not repent. So whether we are speaking of Christian or Messianic believers, corporate Israel, or the unbelievers of the world, the purpose of many great catastrophes of the last days, is to give them the opportunity to repent, and ultimately, to draw closer to the Lord. Although the trials and difficulties are largely the same, it is the reactions that are so drastically different. Believers, and ultimately Israel, will allow the pains of the tribulation to break their will and bring them closer to the Lord. The stubborn, unbending unbelievers will not repent, thus sealing their eternal destiny.

IT'S GOD

This is the great mystery, not only of pain but much more specifically of the last days. Although it would be very easy to look upon that time of unparalleled human suffering and see only the hand of Satan, the truth is the many castrophes of those days will very much be the work of God's hand. In pondering this mystery, I am reminded of two passages, which on the surface seem to be entirely contradictory. In 2 Samuel we are told that the Lord's anger burned against Israel and "he incited David against them, saying, 'Go and take a census of Israel and Judah'" (2 Sam. 24:1). In a parallel passage found in 1 Chronicles, however, we are told that, "Satan stood up against Israel, and moved David to number Israel" (1 Chron. 21:1). So which was it, the Lord or Satan? Again, in the mysterious interplay between the reality of human will (as well as the free will of spiritual beings such as angels or demons) and the reality concerning the absolute sovereignty of God, there is a degree to which both are true. Satan stirred up David's heart to carry out these things, but behind the actions of the devil, the Lord was accomplishing His ultimate will. Such will also be the case as it pertains to the Antichrist, the man who will function essentially as Satan's human puppet in the days to come. It is only by understanding this mysterious interaction between the will of Satan and the much larger will of God that we can rightly understand the activity of the Antichrist in the last days. Consider for example the fact that God will allow the Antichrist to be successful in all he does:

> His power will be mighty, but not by his own power, and he will destroy to an extraordinary degree and prosper and perform his will; he will destroy mighty men and the holy people. And through his shrewdness he will cause deceit to succeed by his influence; and he will magnify himself in his heart, and he will destroy many while they are at ease. (Daniel 8:24-25)

Further, the Lord Himself will actually allow the Antichrist to succeed:

> Then the king will do as he pleases, and he will exalt and magnify himself above every god and will speak monstrous things against the God of gods; and he will prosper until the indignation is finished, for that which is decreed will be done. (Daniel 11:36)

This is why the Antichrist is actually referred to as God's rod of chastisement. In Isaiah 10, the prophet uses the ancient contention between Israel and Assyria as a prototype for the final days of Israel. The language there concerning the Lord's use of an adversarial, hostile, pagan nation as His rod of discipline is essential for us to grasp:

> Woe to Assyria, the rod of My anger and the staff in whose hands is My indignation, I send it against a godless nation and commission it against the people of My fury to capture booty and to seize plunder, and to trample them down like mud in the streets. (Isaiah 10:5-6)

Of course, it should also be mentioned, that after the Lord uses the Antichrist to accomplish His own purposes, He will then break that rod over his knee:

> So it will be that when the Lord has completed all His work on Mount Zion and on Jerusalem, He will say, "I will punish the fruit of the arrogant heart of the king of Assyria and the pomp of his haughtiness." (Isaiah 10:12)

This lesson is critical because beyond invading Israel, we are also told in Revelation 12, that the Antichrist will specifically pursue the destruction, not only of Israel but also Christians, described as those, "who keep the commandments of God and hold to the testimony of Jesus" (Rev. 12:17). When the world is faced with such events, how easy will it be to interpret these things as the failure of God's will. This is the essential take away lesson: The Antichrist and His future success are not some anomalies whereby Satan will come very close to successfully thwarting the Lord's plans. The great tribulation brought on by the Antichrist and his hordes is actually all part of the Lord's perfect plan.

This mysterious interaction between free will and the sovereignty of God has produced endless debates, controversies, and profound divisions within the body of Christ for centuries. Our desire here is most certainly not to revisit or stir up such controversies. Instead, we hope to emphasize the fact that no matter how Satan is working in our midst, God is sovereign and remains in absolute and complete control. Our job as His ambassadors and ministers in the last days is to focus on what God is doing and to do our best to partner with His redemptive purposes.

Now, it must be stated very plainly that although suffering is something that God allows, and even brings into our lives for our own ultimate good, we must be careful never to interpret this to mean that God desires us to suffer. If we are speaking about what God desires in the sense of what he takes delight in, then we may categorically say that our suffering is never His will. We do not want anyone to misinterpret what is being presented here as an argument for what some may interpret as an unloving or abusive God. Nothing could be farther from the truth.

Although the Lord is far more mysterious and transcendent than we will ever be able to fully understand, He has nevertheless chosen, through the Scriptures, to communicate who He is: a God who genuinely and passionately cares about every one of us. The Lord grieves when we grieve, and He hurts for us when we are in pain. The Lord always desires the best for us. He is always good. In his omnipotence and sovereignty, He is able to allow billions of individual human beings and spiritual beings to all live in the same universe, each expressing their own free wills, while still remaining in control of all things. "And we know that God causes all things to work together for good to those who love God, to those who are called according to His purpose" (Romans 8:28). In this age, pain and suffering are unavoidable, yet the Lord will use it for our own eternal good, and for His eternal glory. Our job is to trust Him.

CONCLUSION

As the age of man's rule comes to a close and we transition into a new age governed by righteousness and justice, the Lord has purposed to allow the Antichrist to arise, to bring about an unparalleled time of great tribulation to give all people the opportunity to fall on the rock of ages rather than face the day of judgment when it will fall upon them and grind them to powder (see Matt. 21:44). The Lord will use the coming great catastrophes to bring His people into greater maturity, to make them a people more given to prayer, and to prepare them to meet the glorious Bridegroom. The Lord will also use this time of tribulation to once and for all bring His people Israel into perfect and perpetual covenantal obedience. And finally, He will give the unbelievers of the world one final season of opportunity to repent and turn to Him before the ultimate day of judgment. Understanding all of these things, the mysterious culmination of all redemptive history, it is imperative that we as ambassadors of Christ carefully consider, as we will do in the next chapter, what should be our response to days ahead.

What I did not realize was that standing just behind me was another Syrian man, listening to my prayer. After the prayer, one of those on our team saw the man quickly turn away and walk behind the tent. He followed the man and saw him break down, crying with heaving sobs. He told me, "Nathan, if I had just said the name Jesus, he would have called out to Him with all his heart." He later went back and found the man and prayed for him.

—SYRIAN REFUGEE CRISIS, PERSONAL JOURNAL, OCTOBER 30, 2015

10

OUR RESPONSE

Love your enemies.
—MATTHEW 5:44

MOVING FROM DENIAL TO ACCEPTANCE

In 1969, grief expert Elizabeth Kübler-Ross observed that when we lose a loved one, or any kind of sudden tragedy strikes, we often process our shock and loss through five distinct stages. The first is denial, followed by anger, then bargaining, depression, and finally acceptance. All of these are mechanisms the human heart turns to in order to cope with something that is simply too painful. Having travelled the world for the past dozen or so years, often speaking about the harsh reality concerning radical Islam, and most specifically what the future holds as it pertains to global Islam, I am convinced that the vast majority of the church is still presently locked somewhere between denial and anger.

There are multiple mechanisms through which Christians remain in denial. Within circles given to the study of Bible prophecy, there are various popular theories as to how Islam is going to be removed from holding any place of global influence. This is often envisioned as occurring through an imminent series of prophesied wars. Passages such as Ezekiel 38-39 and Psalm 83 are looked to as support for this. As prophecy teacher David Reagan has commented, "[T]he war of Ezekiel 38 will result in the annihilation of nearly all the armies of the Muslim nations of the Middle East. . . . Thus, if the Antichrist is a Muslim who is going to rule a Muslim empire in the Middle East during the Tribulation, then he is going to rule over an empire that has been reduced to ashes!"[1] Others, primarily within the Charismatic and Pentecostal movements, often speak of such a mighty revival sweeping the Muslim world, that the threat of Islam all but disappears. In both cases, these visions are used as coping mechanisms to help Christians remain in denial. While it is certainly true that there are more Muslims coming to faith right now than at any time in the history of Islam, even if these numbers continue to skyrocket, it is still not going to be enough to make the challenge of radical global Islam simply go away. Likewise, while the Bible does indeed predict divine judgment being leveled against the coming coalition of nations adversarial to Israel, a more careful study of the context of those passages places their judgments at the time of Jesus's return. We are faced with the undeniable reality that a future where radical Islamic terrorism continues to dominate the global landscape remains and where tremendous persecution for Christians is common. As the body of Christ, we must move beyond the phase of denial regarding the relevance and challenge of Islam in the days ahead.

Then there are those who have made the next step into anger. As I travel and speak on the issue of Islam, I find no shortage of Christians who fall into this category. Their primary heart reaction to the topic of Islam or Muslims often borders on rage. Any survey of the caustic comments section of nearly any online article about Islam will produce dozens, if not hundreds, of comments expressing that the best response to the problem of global radical Islam is something along the lines of total extermination. Muslims are far too frequently dehumanized and deemed worthy of only death. These kinds of sentiments are often mingled with ample biblical citations and rhetoric, indicating that many of these comments come from those who view themselves as Christians.

Our hope with this book is that all who read it will come to the final stage of grief—to the place of acceptance. Until the global body of Christ comes to accept the great challenge ahead, they will not be able to begin walking out a Christ-centered response and most certainly will never develop any kind of strategic gospel-centered action plan.

WHERE ARE THE BONHOEFFERS?

I've always greatly admired the foresight of Dietrich Bonhoeffer. During the early days of the rise of Nazism in the 1930s, while most German Christian leaders were silent, Bonhoeffer was boldly warning the German church concerning the dark cloud that was descending over his nation. Despite his foresight and the dark times in which he lived, Bonhoeffer was no doom prophet or wild-eyed alarmist. He was first and foremost a man with a shepherd's heart for God's people who sought to prepare them to live as disciples of Jesus during such an evil era. As then, so also today many Christian leaders are unwilling to truly face or acknowledge what lies ahead. Unlike in Bonhoeffer's day, today there are many voices warning about the rise of radical Islam, but they are functioning much more as doomsday prophets, cursing the darkness but doing very little about it. Few of the voices are from leaders who are soberly aware of what is coming and are also forming a strategy to guide the church through the days ahead. Where are the Dietrich Bonhoeffers of our day? Where are the prophet–shepherds rallying God's people to awaken from their slumber to stand firm, victorious even, as it faces the *last Reich*? Oh that the Lord would raise up an army of wise shepherds, a mighty throng of Bonhoeffers to guide the Lord's people through the time of great trial that is closing in upon us. *This is the great need of the hour!* Although the purpose of this chapter is not so much to lay out an actual strategy, it is in the spirit of Deitrich Bonehoeffer that we hope to lay out a proper Jesus-centered heart response to the current darkness on the immediate horizon.

A CHRIST-CENTERED RESPONSE

As we have repeatedly stated, Islam is now, and will continue to be, the greatest giant to confront the people of God. Until Jesus returns, this Goliath will continue his satanic mocking and taunting of the servants of God. Today, much of the church stands on the opposite hill looking across at the armies of the giant Philistine, afraid and confused to the point of paralysis. Others are simply unsure of how to respond. One thing, however, is clear; we must respond. Just because this Goliath will not ultimately be defeated until Jesus returns, does not mean that we should sit back and do nothing. As we said, the purpose of this chapter, and to a larger degree, of this book, is not primarily to detail a specific strategic action plan, as there are hundreds of various strategies whereby we might respond in a gospel-centered way to the rise of Islam. Again, the primary purpose here is to discuss the proper Jesus-centered heart response. How should we be directing our emotions, our heart, our energy, and our prayers in the face of such a colossal challenge? For some, the natural response is to somewhat passively await the return of Jesus for deliverance. For others, it is to take a more active posture, confronting Islam through activism, the legal system, or even militarily. None of these responses is entirely wrong. Indeed, we as followers of Jesus should eagerly yearn for the return of Jesus. It is also right for Christians to engage the world through political activism and at times, even support their governments when they engage evildoers with the sword of justice. The real issue here is first determining where our priorities lie and second what a proper Christ-centered heart posture should be toward the challenge of Islam. If we can get these two issues right, then the amount of energy that we direct toward these two matters will naturally regulate. Thankfully, in determining both the posture of our hearts and where our priorities should lie Jesus has already shown us the way, having both taught and demonstrated these things while He was here on the earth. As followers of Jesus, we are called to imitate His example and to implement the things that He taught.

IMITATING JESUS: EMBRACING THE CROSS

It is easy to say that we as Christians are called to follow Jesus, but rarely do we know what that means in our daily lives. Let's consider what following Jesus means specifically as it relates to the growing challenge of radical Islam around the world.

In the Gospel of Luke we find an amazing verse that might easily be missed if we do not pay careful attention to the details. Jesus, knowing full well that betrayal, mutilation, and finally a cross awaited him, said, "When the days drew near for him to be taken up, he set his face to go to Jerusalem" (Luke 9:51, ESV). The King James version says that, "he *steadfastly* set his face." Jesus was not simply ready for what was about to befall Him; He was actually steadfastly determined to embrace the cross. With eyes wide open, Jesus pushed forward toward the day of His execution. Only a few verses earlier Jesus had quite directly revealed to His disciples what awaited Him in Jerusalem, explaining, "The Son of Man must suffer many things and be rejected by the elders and chief priests and scribes, and be killed and be raised up on the third day" (v. 22). Then He immediately issued what is arguably one of the most difficult challenges that Jesus ever issued to His disciples: "If anyone wishes to come after Me, he must deny himself, and take up his cross daily and follow Me" (v. 23).

The conclusion is undeniable. Anyone who desires to follow Jesus must also willingly embrace their own martyrdom. For clarity, this is not to say that we as Christians should deliberately pursue martyrdom. By no means. We are not to be *suicidal*. On the other hand, Jesus made it clear that we shouldn't deliberately seek a safe and comfortable life. Quite the contrary: "For whoever wishes to save his life will lose it, but whoever loses his life for My sake, he is the one who will save it" (v 24). Everything in this world screams, "save yourself!" This is largely why Paul spoke of, "the offense of the cross" (Gal. 5:11, NIV). No one naturally enjoys suffering, relishes in making great sacrifices, or even desires to die. Yet this is precisely what the Lord has called us to set our faces steadfastly toward. If this calling potentially involves our own death, then so be it. We are not those who live in fear of death, rather we are those who lay down our lives for the sake of others.

To up the ante, even more than placing others first, Jesus actually laid down His life *for His enemies*. As Paul the apostle reminds us:

> Christ died for the ungodly. For one will hardly die for a righteous man; though perhaps for the good man someone would dare even to die. But God demonstrates His own love toward us, in that while we were yet sinners, Christ died for us. (Romans 5:6-8)

Likewise, we also are called to lay down our lives for our enemies. Jesus commands us to "love your enemies and pray for those who persecute you" (Matt. 5:44), and again He calls us to "love your enemies, do good to those who hate you" (Luke 6:27). The reason is simple. The Scriptures teach that, "while we were enemies we were reconciled to God through the death of His Son" (Rom. 5:10). Since the Lord has, "committed to us the word of reconciliation" (2 Cor. 5:19), it is our job to pursue the reconciliation of God's enemies. As Jesus treated us, we are to treat others. If the message of the cross was offensive before, then how much more offensive is it when we realize that the Lord calls us to actually lay down our lives for our enemies?

THE MARTYR AND THE MURDERER

There was a very religious Jew, a leader in his community. This man was simply infuriated by the growing Messianic Jewish movement that was spreading throughout Israel. Among the new messianic believers was a young man who was very passionate about his faith. He had become a deacon in his local congregation and was a truly shining example of a young man filled with the Holy Spirit. The young man also had a gift for sharing the gospel with his fellow countrymen who lived in and around Jerusalem. The young man was so effective in his public proclamation of the truth that the older religious Jewish leader felt that he had to confront him. He took a group of men from the religious community and actually murdered the young man in cold blood, in the streets of

Jerusalem. It was a horrific event that reverberated through the messianic community. Here was this shining-faced, vibrant, young believer whose skull was literally crushed simply because of his faith. While the older man who instigated the murder didn't actually cast any of the stones, as the Bible indicates, he did stand there, holding the coats of the others who did, all the while giving his hearty approval. The gifted young man who was filled with the Holy Spirit was Stephen. And the man who stirred up the persecutors was Saul, who later became known as Paul, the apostle.

It's shocking that the Lord specifically chose to use a man who was formerly a murderer, seeking to terrorize the relatively young community of Jesus followers. But this was indeed God's choice. This was the man who the Lord picked to redeem and then use to pen much of the New Testament. This was the man whom the Lord chose to give apostolic, fatherly leadership to so many of the early churches throughout the ancient Mediterranean world. If the Lord could use a zealot like Paul, essentially a terrorist, then how can we say that all terrorists are beyond His reach today? How can any Christian ever suggest that the only solution for the problem of radical Muslims is annihilation? This is not to say that Christians need to oppose military operations to destroy terrorist cells or militant groups. The Lord has given the mandate to governments to wield the sword and protect its people. The point here is to emphasize the *primary* calling of followers of Jesus as it pertains to the rise of global terrorism. Our job is to seek the salvation of as many as possible, not to seek their destruction.

The more that Satan seeks to raise up an army of his own from among the spiritual sons of Ishmael, so should followers of Jesus make it their priority to snatch as many Muslims from the fires of hell as possible. Now is not the moment to make self-preservation our highest priority. Now is the hour when Christians across the globe must rise up to give ourselves to see Muslims come to faith. We are called to rescue Muslims from God's wrath because that is what Jesus did for us.

SNATCH THEM FROM THE FIRE!

On October 12, 2002—just a little more than a year after 9/11—there was another large-scale terrorist attack in Bali, Indonesia. At that time, I had been engaged in a lengthy e-mail dialogue with a young Muslim convert from England named Jimmy. The terrorist attack at the Sari Club, a popular tourist hang-out, resulted in the death of 202 people. Another 209 were injured. What shocked me at that time was the incredibly cold manner in which Jimmy supported the terrorist attack. According to his reasoning, because the victims were not Muslims, they essentially got what they deserved. I suggested to Jimmy that there was a good chance some of the two hundred or so mostly young people would have converted to Islam sometime during their lifetimes. Would it not be more reasonable, I asked, for him, as a Muslim, to be opposed to their killing and instead seek to convert them? "Wouldn't you wish to save as many as possible, rather than send them to an eternity in hell?" I asked. But according to Jimmy, the purpose of Islam is not to save as many as possible from the torments of hell, rather its purpose is to establish shari'ah—Allah's laws, according to Islam—on the earth. According to Jimmy's rationale, the public killing of these "infidels," would do much more to help establish the fear of Allah, and thus a willingness to submit to his laws, than would a few converts to Islam. He had no compassion for those who were murdered. It was through that conversation that I gained a much deeper understanding of the difference between the god of Islam and my God. The god of Islam, it seems, has his priorities set on establishing his dominance over as many as possible, with very little concern for those who are lost in the process. The God of the Bible said, "The thief comes only to steal and kill and destroy; I came that they may have life, and have it abundantly" (John 10:10). The God of the Bible actually laments those who are wayward, appealing to them to come to Him to find life: "'As I live!' declares the Lord God, 'I take no pleasure in the death of the wicked, but rather that the wicked turn from his way and live. Turn back, turn back from your evil ways! Why then will you die?'" (Ez. 33:11). Jesus, who is the very essence of God in the flesh, was very clear in stating His priorities:

The Son of Man has come to save that which was lost. "What do you think? If any man has a hundred sheep, and one of them has gone astray, does he not leave the ninety-nine on the mountains and go and search for the one that is straying? If it turns out that he finds it, truly I say to you, he rejoices over it more than over the ninety-nine which have not gone astray. So it is not the will of your Father who is in heaven that one of these little ones perish." (Matthew 18:11-14)

The implications are clear. Saving lives, saving souls, is God's priority. Since this is the very nature of our God, so also should we imitate and represent Him. Our mandate in this age is not to act like the god of Islam or any of his more radicalized followers, seeking to send as many Muslim terrorists as possible to their death. No! For, "the Son of Man did not come to destroy men's lives, but to save them" (Luke 9:56). So also should we make it our priority to save souls. Our job as followers of Jesus is to snatch as many from the fire as we can. In this age, we are to partner with our God in His grand rescue mission.

On the first Sunday following the tragedy of September 11, 2001, Carter Conlon, pastor of Times Square Church in Manhattan preached a sermon titled "Run for Your Life." It is one of the most moving sermons I have ever heard, and I encourage everyone to look it up on YouTube and listen to the sermon in its entirety. Here is a portion of the sermon:

> Listen to me like you've never listened to me ever in your life. . . . My mind is forever branded with the stories that I heard of police officers from the city of New York. As people were fleeing from a crumbling building, there were police officers and firemen and others who were running towards the buildings saying, "Run for your life," even at their own peril. And in some cases, I believe they knew they were going to die, but there was a sense of duty. I was crying out to God, I said, "God, oh Jesus, don't let my sense of duty be less for Your Kingdom than these beloved firemen and policemen were for those who were perishing in a falling tower. We're living in a generation

when truth is falling into the streets. I want to be among those who are not running away from the conflict, but running into the conflict and saying, "Run for your life!"

This is the kind of response that the last-days church must learn to embody. This is the kind of spirit in which the Lord calls all of His people to walk. This is, after all, the very kind of spirit that God Himself demonstrated to the world when He willingly took on flesh and allowed Himself to be mutilated in order to save us, His enemies. Perhaps no other passage in the Bible better captures our call to follow Jesus' example of self-sacrifice than Philippians 2:

> Do nothing from selfishness or empty conceit, but with humility of mind regard one another as more important than yourselves; do not merely look out for your own personal interests, but also for the interests of others. Have this attitude in yourselves which was also in Christ Jesus, who, although He existed in the form of God, did not regard equality with God a thing to be grasped, but emptied Himself, taking the form of a bond-servant, and being made in the likeness of men. Being found in appearance as a man, He humbled Himself by becoming obedient to the point of death, even death on a cross. (Philippians 2:3-8)

Oh Lord, help us to become genuine imitators of your Son!

LIVING AS A COMMUNITY OF THE CROSS

If the body of Christ is to respond properly to the rise of radical Islam, then it is essential that we become a people who embody the message of the cross. The church, at its heart, is intended to be a community of the cross. What does this mean? It means that as a people, we lay down our lives, not only for one another but even for our enemies. The message of the cross is the message of the mercy of God to sinners. While preaching the message of the cross is critical, living it is even more critical.

It is essential to recognize that Islam is not a culture of the cross.

Islam is a religion whose prophet followed the self-seeking pattern of the world. Muhammad may have used a veneer of religious piety and mission, but his goals were those of any other self-seeking, self-glorifying, self-obsessed individual. In other words, Islam preaches what the world already understands. In the gospel of Mark, Jesus described the nature of the world. He called His disciples together and explained to them, "You know that those who are recognized as rulers of the Gentiles lord it over them; and their great men exercise authority over them" (Mark 10:42). The way of the world is to strive to attain positions of authority in order to "lord it over" others. While every position of authority known to man is intended to be a position of servant leadership, instead, far too often, when men and woman secure positions for themselves, they use them to empower themselves, even if it means doing so at the expense of others. Again, this is no different within Islam. Muhammad didn't model a life of servant leadership and certainly did not teach Muslims to lay down their lives for others. The god of the Qur'an does not demonstrate or communicate a self-sacrificial love. This is precisely why the witness of individual Christians and Christian communities who model the cross to Muslims speaks so powerfully. It communicates the very nature of the true God who Muslims yearn to know. When Christian communities reflect the nature of God in this regard, we are proclaiming the truth of what God is like through our actions. Many former Muslims I have spoken with say that the primary pivotal issue that won them over to Christ was that a Christian or Christians loved them unconditionally. This is the kind of love that can win over even the most deceived or hardened heart. Individual Christians and Christian communities must learn how to treat others as God Himself has treated them. By living this way, especially as the darkness increases, our light and witness for Christ will shine the brightest.

BECOMING A COMMUNITY OF PRAYER
Another critical issue, which is far too often overlooked by many Christians, is the necessity to become a community of prayer. This is,

after all, what the Father intended for His church. As it is written in the prophet Isaiah, "My house will be called a house of prayer for all the peoples" (Isa. 56:7). Isaiah's reference was to the temple in Jerusalem, which we as the body of Christ are a spiritual, corporate expression of (see Eph. 2:21). The spiritual landscape of the last days will be dominated by two primary houses of prayer on the earth: The body of Christ and the House of Islam. Currently numbering at roughly 1.8 billion, Muslims tend to be, among all the peoples on the earth, the most committed to prayer. It is quite unlikely that a devout Muslim who prays five times a day will leave his religion to join a new religious community that prays much less than he did as a Muslim. If the body of Christ is serving the true God, shouldn't we be a people far more committed to prayer than those who are serving the false god of Islam? If the people of God ever expect to confront this last great Goliath, then it will only be done after we as a global community commit ourselves to truly living as a house of prayer for all peoples.

DEMONSTRATION OF THE CROSS

Although we've already discussed the need to follow Christ and lay down our lives—even for our enemies—we cannot conclude this chapter without taking this discussion a step further and talk specifically about martyrdom. The Greek word *martus* is translated as "martyr" and simply means "witness." The early church had a solid understanding of the role of martyrdom in fulfilling its mandate to bear witness to the world. This was one of its great strengths that propelled it to become a movement that would turn the ancient world upside down in a very short period of time. Today, the modern church has all but lost a theology of martyrdom, particularly in the Western world. They will recover it, however.

Although Christian martyrdom has always been part of the story of the church, Jesus was quite clear that it will reach its culmination and pinnacle in the last days. In His Olivet Discourse, a sermon dedicated exclusively to the end times, Jesus told His followers what to expect during that time: "you will be handed over to be persecuted and put to death, and you will be hated by all nations because of me" (Matthew 24:9, NIV). In the book of Revelation, we are told that when the Antichrist and False Prophet arise, they will be given the authority to kill anyone who does not submit to their religious worship system (see Rev. 13:15). Elsewhere in Revelation, we are informed that this great number of martyrs will largely be killed through beheading:

> I saw thrones on which were seated those who had been given authority to judge. And I saw the souls of those who had been beheaded because of their testimony for Jesus and because of the word of God. They had not worshiped the beast or his image and had not received his mark on their foreheads or their hands. They came to life and reigned with Christ a thousand years. (Revelation 20:4, NIV)

What is so essential to grasp here, is that the martyrdom of Christians, which will reach its peak across the earth in the last days, is all part of the Lord's perfect plan. In fact, in another passage in Revelation, we are told that the end will not come, until the full number of martyrs is completed:

> And there was given to each of them a white robe; and they were told that they should rest for a little while longer, until the number of their fellow servants and their brethren who were to be killed even as they had been, would be completed also. (Revelation 6:11)

At the time of this writing, according to the Christian organization Open Doors, Christian persecution is at its all-time high.[2] We must understand that this is not some temporary setback that must be overcome. Rather, we are presently in the early stages of the completion of God's perfect plan. This is a mystery that the church must understand. The Lord has a very important purpose for end-time martyrdom. It is through a great multitude of faithful witnesses who will, like their master, willingly lay down their lives for their enemies that the Lord will give a final glorious witness to all the world concerning the message of the cross, His offer of mercy to sinners. It is specifically through

Christian martyrdom that the Lord will give the inhabitants of the world one final opportunity to receive the mercy of God and repent before the day of judgment. This then will be the nature of the church in the last days. They will be a people committed to declaring the eternal gospel to all of mankind as final witness, *and then the end will come.*

CONCLUSION

In order for the church to rise to meet the great challenge of Islam both now and in the days ahead, we must first be willing to accept the reality that until Jesus returns, Islam, and the global persecution that accompanies it, is not going away. As difficult as it is, the increasing persecution and martyrdom of Christians is the new normal. All of these things were foretold in the Scriptures. Once we come to terms with this reality, then we may join hands in a unified response that is entirely rooted in the imitation of Jesus. This will be a response that prioritizes the proclamation of the gospel, the salvation of the lost to those who are perishing without knowing God. It will be a response that takes seriously the call to imitate Jesus by laying down our lives, even for our enemies. Our response will be to join hands in the greatest rescue mission in redemptive history. Finally, it will be a response that understands the Lord's purpose for the martyrdom of His saints, that of bearing witness concerning the mercy of God to all mankind. In responding this way, we will fulfill the Lord's mandate to His people in the increasingly difficult and challenging days ahead.

Part 3

HOW THEN SHALL WE RESPOND?

(Nathan Graves)

Dear Lord, help me to not be afraid to look at the suffering of the Syrian refugees. I need you to do this in me, Lord. I don't want to see more. It's too hard. I don't want to imagine the horrors and I don't want to give any more of myself than what I've given to help them. I'm tired and I want to enjoy happy things. It's all too sad. But I know, Lord, there is nothing more important to you. The pain of their suffering now was the pain of your suffering then, when you gave your life on the cross for each of them. You know the trauma of every anguished heart and you bore the loss of every weeping soul. Your eye is fixed steadfast on each one and your hand outstretched to save them. So, Lord, may I, on behalf of them, enter into the fellowship of your sufferings. Give me grace and strength so that they may see You, and in You, find comfort in their tragedy and salvation for their eternal souls. In Jesus name, Amen.

—SYRIAN REFUGEE CRISIS PERSONAL JOURNAL, FEBRUARY 29, 2016

11

THE GRAND CLIMAX

The Father loves the Son and has given all things into His Hand.

—JOHN 3:35

UNLESS WE ARE ABLE to follow the whole story of catastrophe in the Bible, from beginning to end, it will be difficult to comprehend why things will unfold as they will in the last days. However, if we keep in mind that the goal of God is to fill the earth with His glory in the salvation of some from every nation, which He will one day hand to His Son as His long-awaited inheritance, then it will make sense. God is moving everything in heaven and on earth to this final victorious conclusion. Just as God has used catastrophe as His primary means of determining the movements of man across the globe since Adam was cast out of the garden, He will continue to do so until the last crisis befalls the human race and every ethnic group is brought into the fold of God.

This is both His story and ours. It is an incredibly amazing account of God that we get to be a part of in the last days. Think of it this way.

More than two thousand years ago, Jesus gave His disciples His last command to make disciples of all nations by declaring the good news of His death, burial and resurrection to the whole world. This was the first generation of ambassadors Jesus sent out to share this message globally. Since that time hundreds of generations have come and gone over the centuries and still the mission is not complete. But just as Jesus raised up a first generation of emissaries to fulfill His mandate, He will raise up a last generation to finish the task before His return. *Could it be that God has reserved us to be that generation?!* If so, we have been given the high privilege, holy honor, and the massive responsibility to complete the greatest mission ever given to man.

This possibility increases exponentially the urgency of the call to preach the gospel. We have reached an emergency level. It is like the building pressure of a massive volcano. Tremors and warning signs are given before the volcano erupts. The biblical narrative is coming to a grand climax. In its concluding narrative, the earth will experience natural and man-made disasters the likes of which have never been witnessed before. A global eruption is about to take place, literally, and we need to get ready. Billions of people are living their lives with no knowledge of what is about to be unleashed. It may very well be that God has determined our times to be the time of the end to make one last push for salvation of the unreached nations of the earth.

CATASTROPHE AND THE FINAL REVIVAL

When it is suggested that the greatest revival ever will unfold in the last days, many are quick to point out the many passages that speak about the negative aspects of the tribulation. They point out that the primary emphasis of Jesus and the apostles concerns an end-times apostasy (see 2 Thess. 2:3), the love of most growing cold, (see Matt. 24:12), a strong delusion (see 2 Thess. 2:11), the abundance of false prophets and false christs (see Matt. 24:4-5, 11, 24; Mark 13:6; Luke 21:8; Rev. 13:11-14; 16:13; 19-20; 20:10), and spiritual deception getting worse (see 2 Tim. 3:13). All this is true. The reality concerning these things in no way precludes a great end-times revival as well. In fact, the Scriptures are clear that in the last days there will be both a great falling away as well as a great outpouring of the Holy Spirit. In no way are the two exclusive. What is the scriptural basis for an end-time revival? A starting point would most certainly be Joel 2:

> It will come about after this that I will pour out My Spirit on all mankind; and your sons and daughters will prophesy, your old men will dream dreams, your young men will see visions. Even on the male and female servants I will pour out My Spirit in those days. I will display wonders in the sky and on the earth, blood, fire and columns of smoke. The sun will be turned into darkness and the moon into blood before the great and awesome day of the LORD comes. And it will come about that whoever calls on the name of the LORD will be delivered; for on Mount Zion and in Jerusalem there will be those who escape, as the LORD has said, even among the survivors whom the LORD calls. (Joel 2:28-32)

There are those who argue that because Peter applied this passage to the outpouring in the first century at Pentecost that it has been completely fulfilled and has no bearing on the last days. Such an argument not only must ignore the clear language concerning the cosmic signs and the day of the Lord, but it also misunderstands the concept of fulfillment. There are many interim fulfillments of various prophecies but only one ultimate day of the Lord. At Pentecost, the cosmic signs were not fulfilled. The sun did not turn dark, nor did the moon become like blood. This passage will be ultimately fulfilled in the season before the day of the Lord. Throughout history there have been many antichrists, but there's only one ultimate Antichrist. Throughout history, there have been many seasons of tribulation, but there is only one great tribulation (see Deut. 32; Jer. 30; Dan. 12; Matt. 24). There have been many outpourings of the Holy Spirit, but Scripture only speaks of one great end-time outpouring: "And it shall be in the last days, says God, "that I will pour out my spirit on all people" (see Acts 2:17).

Other passages reveal a localized last-days revival. In Isaiah 19 we are told that Egypt will come under the hand of a "cruel master" and a "mighty king" (v. 4). Beyond this, the Nile will dry up, the economy will be desolated, and Egypt will cry out to the Lord (v. 20). The prophecy goes on to describe the Lord responding to them and bringing revival to the land:

> Thus the LORD will make Himself known to Egypt, and the Egyptians will know the LORD in that day. They will even worship with sacrifice and offering, and will make a vow to the LORD and perform it. The LORD will strike Egypt, striking but healing; so they will return to the LORD, and He will respond to them and will heal them. (vv 21-22)

The number of believers in Egypt will be so great that it says that Egypt will come to know the Lord. Isaiah goes on to describe a mighty throng of faithful believers from Assyria. During the age of Messiah, these believers will all be partners with Israel in worshipping the Lord:

> In that day there will be a highway from Egypt to Assyria, and the Assyrians will come into Egypt and the Egyptians into Assyria, and the Egyptians will worship with the Assyrians. In that day Israel will be the third party with Egypt and Assyria, a blessing in the midst of the earth, whom the LORD of hosts has blessed, saying, "Blessed is Egypt My people, and Assyria the work of My hands, and Israel My inheritance." (24-25)

Some may argue that these all come to faith after Jesus returns, but because so much of the prophecy unfolds before His return, we have good reason to believe that the "coming to know the Lord" begins before His return.

In Isaiah 60, during the age of Messiah, we see a multitude of worshippers going up to Jerusalem from the regions of Kedar and Midian (see v.6). This is modern day Saudi Arabia. Others from Lebanon are bringing gifts to beautify the temple at Jerusalem. Once again it is unlikely that this vast multitude all come to faith exclusively after His return. In fact, another reason to believe that there will be a great revival throughout the Middle East is because it is already happening. There are more Muslims coming to faith now than at any other time in history.[1]

Beyond promises of a great number of believers coming to faith in Jesus in certain regions, there are other hints of a great last-days revival. In Revelation 7 we see not only the 144,000 Jewish believers (there are only around twenty thousand Messianic believers in Israel today) but also a great multitude that came out of the tribulation. Depending on which position one holds concerning the timing of the rapture, they will interpret the identify of these individuals differently. Either way however, it is a vast number of believers from every tongue, tribe, and people group. Concerning this number of believers, I find myself in full agreement with Dr. R. L. Hymers Jr., a conservative premillennialist Baptist preacher who rejoices in the revival that is coming, even during the time of the great apostasy:

> But there is a bright spot in this dark and horrible time. Our deacon, Dr. Chan, read the prophecy of this in Revelation 7:1-14 a moment ago. *That bright spot in the Tribulation period is the greatest revival of true Christianity that the world has ever seen!* Revivals have often been sent by God in times of great trouble and apostasy.[2]

As we have already discussed, the Lord always uses catastrophe to bring about redemption. Why would we expect it to be any different in the last days? Understanding the central role of cataclysm throughout redemptive history, we should be expecting God to continue to do what He has consistently done in the past. As a result of these future tribulations, we should also expect to see many more people turn to Christ before His return. Throughout history, God has claimed multitudes for His glory and brought them into His kingdom through global disasters. But the greatest revival to occur among the nations as a result of catastrophe is yet to come. It will be a revival of epic proportions, making the First and Second Great Awakenings pale in comparison.

THE CORONATION AND PROMISE

Over this past quarter century my wife and I have pursued one specific aim as expressed in our ministry's positioning statement: Discovering innovative paths to the least-reached. This idea has been the catalyst for all of our pioneering efforts since 1979 when God led me to an unreached people. Since then, the unreached have been our passion. But why go to the unreached? Why would God place such a heavy burden on the heart of a teenage boy for a people I had never heard of? Why, with all of the places in the world to go, would God send any of us to the remotest parts of the earth? The obvious answer is that God sent His Son to die for the sins of the world (see John 3:16). But sometimes the obvious obscures a larger, grander reality.

I have always understood missions as God's plan to save mankind from the curse of sin, to rescue him from the penalty of hell and to restore him back into a right relationship with Himself. This is true. It is the gospel of Jesus Christ that saves us (see 1 Cor. 15: 1-4; Rom. 1:16). This is the message we preach. But why does God save mankind through the foolishness of preaching (see 1 Cor. 1:21)?

Why would God be so passionate about His gospel message being preached throughout the whole world, through His weak and failing servants to lost, rebellious sinners? It is for His glory that He may be worshipped by all nations. It is to reveal His power and His love to His creation. But is there more to it? I believe so, and that "more to it" has led us to redefine missions. It comes down to a promise made from a Father to His Son. In the twelve verses of Psalm 2 a coronation ceremony is taking place in which a new King is being proclaimed and anointed by God to the world. In this messianic psalm we see that one day the world will recognize this King as the One who will rule the nations of the earth. During the course of the coronation ceremony the newly anointed King says, "I will surely tell of the decree of the LORD: He said to Me, 'Thou art My Son, today I have begotten Thee'" (Ps. 2:7). In Paul's address to the Jews in Pisidian, Antioch, he said, "And we preach to you the good news of the promise made to the fathers, that

God has fulfilled this promise to our children in that He raised up Jesus, as it is also written in the second Psalm, 'Though art My Son; today I have begotten Thee.' As for the fact that He raised Him up from the dead, no more to return to decay, He has spoken in this way: 'I will give you the holy and sure blessings of David'" (Acts 13:32-34). The expression, "today I have begotten Thee" is a reference to the resurrection of Jesus Christ from the dead. It is in His resurrection that Jesus received His authority as the Son of God. It is not that He *becomes* the Son at that moment, but rather He receives His authority as the Son to make His kingly request to the Father recorded in Psalm 2.

In verse eight of this chapter, the Lord says to His newly anointed and resurrected King, "Ask of Me, and I will surely give the nations as Your inheritance, and the very ends of the earth as Your possession" (Ps. 2:8).

Now in Jesus' resurrection, and in His mediatorial office, He becomes the sovereign head of His church. He completely fulfilled all that the Father had commissioned Him to do and obeyed Him to the end. Now, in this royal crowning moment, Jesus rightfully receives the authority to make His grand request for the nations to the Father.

Adam Clarke says: "Having died as an atoning sacrifice, and risen again from the dead, he was now to make intercession for mankind; and in virtue and on account of what he had done and suffered, he was, at his request, to have the nations for his inheritance, and the uttermost parts of the earth for his possession."[3]

This is proven in Paul's letter to the Romans:

> Concerning His Son, who was descended from David according to the flesh, and was declared to be the Son of God in power according to the Spirit of holiness by his resurrection from the dead, Jesus Christ our Lord, through whom we have received grace and apostleship to bring about the obedience of faith for the sake of his name among the nations. (Romans 1:3-5, ESV)

THE COMMISSION

Jesus, having fulfilled all the Father had given Him to do, at the very moment of His resurrection, could have turned to the Father and asked Him for what rightfully belonged to Him: the nations of the earth. Instead, He does something absolutely stunning and beyond human comprehension. Rather than turning to the Father and asking Him for His long-awaited inheritance, He turns to His small band of timid disciples and commissions them to go out and deliver His inheritance—the nations of the earth—to Him:

> And Jesus came up and spoke to them, saying, "All authority has been given to Me in heaven and on earth. Go therefore and make disciples of all nations, baptizing them in the name of the Father and the Son and the Holy Spirit." (Matthew 28:18-19)

Why didn't Jesus commission His disciples before the resurrection? The reason is clear. He had not yet received His authority as the Son to make His grand request to the Father. That authority was given to Jesus when He was resurrected from the dead. But instead of asserting that resurrection authority and making His claim for the nations directly to the Father, Jesus commissions His disciples to go and deliver the nations to Him.

Imagine the responsibility! Imagine the privilege! Imagine the risk! This promise of the nations, made by the Father to the Son was also initiated by the Father to His Son: *"Ask of Me, and I will surely give you."* Jesus, who had so faithfully fulfilled all that the Father asked Him to do, was now entrusting to this ragtag group of men this final request of His Father.

It is the Father who loves the world and sent His Son to be a ransom for many. It is the Father who asks for the nations. It is the Son who loves the Father and does all that the Father has commanded. It is the Son who wins the right to possess the nations as His reward. It is the Son who commands His disciples to go. It is the church, all who are a part of His body, who has been given the task to bring in all that Jesus has gained.

THE PRIZE

This promise for all the heathen nations of the earth, made by our heavenly Father to Jesus Christ, the Son, should reveal a glorious truth. The Father will give to His Son everything He has promised. And Jesus will fulfill this last request His Father has asked Him.

On that day when all is said and done, will Jesus receive His prize, His inheritance, and the fruit of His reward? In God's Revelation to John we are given the answer as we are given a glimpse into the future. John sees a book in the right hand of the One who sits on the throne. Then a strong angel proclaims, "Who is worthy to open the book and to break its seals?" (Rev. 5:2). Because no one was worthy to open or look into the book, John weeps greatly. Then one of the elders tells him to stop weeping because the Lion of the Tribe of Judah, the Root of David has overcome so as to open the book. And there between the throne and the elder is a Lamb who had been slain. The Lamb comes and takes the book out of the right hand (symbolizing authority) of Him who sat on the throne. When the Lamb takes the book, the four living creatures and twenty-four elders fall down before the Lamb.

In light of what we've seen regarding the promise the Father made to the Son in Psalm 2, it becomes clear that the book or scroll the Lamb receives in His right hand is the title deed to the nations of the earth. Standing in the midst, the Lamb, as the Redeemer and Mediator, finally receives His reward. Then, when the book is handed to Him, all of those from every tribe, tongue, people and nation fall down and worship the Lamb. And they sing the song of redemption.

Though billions who have rejected salvation in Christ will not be there, most certainly there will be represented there on that day at least one from every ethnic people group. Not one will be missing.

THE INHERITANCE

What glorious truths! But it still does not answer the question of *why* Jesus asks us to gather in what He has already won. The reason is simple and profound. We are His body, and as His body we are "fellow heirs with Christ, if indeed we suffer with Him so that we may also be glorified with Him" (Rom. 8:17).

If we are fellow heirs with Jesus Christ, He wants us to participate in all that He will jointly share with us. Just as we share in His sufferings and the riches of salvation, we will also inherit and rule the nations with Him one day (see Rev. 20:6). This is why the Great Commission is not just for a select few. It is a privilege and responsibility given to all of us. In the power of the Spirit, we get to deliver into the hands of our Savior what He gave His life to gain. Then after the nations are won to Him, He shares His prize with us in His kingdom.

THE MISSION

Today we operate with a new understanding and definition of God's mission in the world: *"The Church delivering to Christ His inheritance."* We've never been more enthusiastic about the task before us. We've never been more enthralled about the vital role of the church in the world. With it has come a deeper and clearer understanding of our Savior's love and majesty. It has also brought a greater awareness of why Satan would want to hinder God's people from fulfilling this mission to the nations. You see, the Great Commission was not only the last command Jesus gave before He ascended to His Father. It is also a promise not yet fulfilled between the Father and the Son. He is depending on us. Until the day when all nations fall down in worship to the Lamb, Satan will use every means at his disposal to destroy God's mission and deny our Savior His reward. The grand story of salvation will not be finished until that moment.

God's call to the church is so much bigger and more important than most of us have ever realized. We can no longer place missions on the margins of our church life. If God's preeminent plan is for us to gather in what remains of the fruit of His labors, so that He might receive His inheritance, nothing should rise above or distract us from this single-minded pursuit. God's people remain to finish the job and will remain until it is done.

It is God who enables. He fits us for the tasks as we yield ourselves to Him. Often God plants us in places where we never trained to be. God is going to get the glory for His work. When we are placed in situations where we feel completely incapable or incompetent, it is there that God is most glorified, because we were forced to cling to Him in total dependency. My ministry or abilities or giftings are not the things which glorify God the most. I can be living like the devil and exercise all of these. But when I am asked to do something I've never done before, for which I have no human ability, I can make excuses or fall into the able hands of my Savior.

—KOSOVAR REFUGEE CRISIS, PERSONAL JOURNAL, APRIL 18, 1999

RISING TO THE TIMES

But you, O Lord, are a God merciful and gracious, slow to anger and abounding in steadfast love and faithfulness.

—PSALM 86:15, ESV

ONE OF THE CLEAR HALLMARKS of catastrophes is that they open opportunities to reach people for Christ in ways that cannot be imagined under normal circumstances. When lives are torn apart by disaster, and when they have lost everything, they are humbled by their experiences. People in these circumstances are much more willing to receive help and to listen.

When encountering refugees, it is fairly easy to identify which ones are true refugees, who are fleeing war or persecution, and those who are taking advantage of the situation to get out of their country by posing as refugees. The ones who are posing are generally proud, loud, and demand to be treated a certain way. The true refugee, who has been traumatized by his or her experiences, is generally quiet, listens, follows instructions, and does not put up a fight. He knows that he and his family are in a frantic situation and is thankful for any help he can get.

There are some who would say that it is insensitive to "preach" to people in these conditions. This is not true. The greatest act of compassion a true follower of Jesus can give to another soul is the life-giving message of salvation in Jesus Christ. Most of the testimonies we have heard throughout our Christian lives, including our own, have come from those who saw their need for a Savior when they were at their lowest and most desperate points in life. It is hard to get any lower or more desperate than to be a distressed, exhausted, and broken refugee. But this is right where many people need to be before they will see their own helplessness before God, and to understand their need for His grace and mercy. It is when Christians show up demonstrating genuine love, compassion and the joy of the Lord, that it is hard for many of them to resist. When Christians stop to talk with refugees, help them, listen to their stories, and show them they really care, it restores a degree of dignity so important to their sense of value and purpose.

The following is a journal entry I made after speaking in a church in Thessaloniki, Greece. It is of a Greek Christian's encounter with a Syrian refugee whose humbling experiences opened his heart to the gospel, and how his experience led to him sharing this same message with Syrian children:

> After I gave my message in the church in Thessaloniki, a Greek brother came up to me and said, "I must tell you a story about a Syrian man who came to faith in Christ through a micro-SD card!" The Syrian man around twenty six escaped the war and has been in a camp in Greece for a year. Alone, without his family, he experienced deep sadness and depression. Some of the Greek Christians tried to encourage him, and little by little he started becoming hopeful. They gave him a micro-SD card and shared the love of Christ with him. His heart was open, and he began attending the church. He was very excited when he saw the film about Jesus. One day in the camp, this Syrian man was trying to get some rest, but about ten boys around ten years old

were playing loudly outside his tent. He went outside and asked them to be quiet. Being boys, they kept making noise, so the man went out a second time and more sternly told them to be quiet. After going in the second time, he thought about how he could quiet them down long enough so he could get some rest. He went outside a third time and said, "Come inside, I want to show you something." He then sat all the boys down, propped his cell phone up on a chair and began playing the film about Jesus in Arabic. The boys immediately quieted down and became transfixed by the movie, which allowed the man to rest quietly. When the movie was finished, the boys rushed outside, and began shouting "Jesus! Jesus! Jesus!" throughout the camp.

But when the chief priests and the teachers of the law saw the wonderful things He did and the children who were shouting in the temple, "Hosanna to the Son of David," they became indignant. "Do you hear what these children are saying?" And Jesus said to them, "Yes; have you never read, 'Out of the mouth of infants and nursing babes You have prepared praise for Yourself'?" (Matthew 21:15-16)

When he came near the place where the road goes down the Mount of Olives, the whole crowd of disciples began joyfully to praise God in loud voices for all the miracles they had seen: "Blessed is the king who comes in the name of the Lord!". . . Some of the Pharisees in the crowd said to Jesus, "Teacher, rebuke your disciples!" "I tell you," he replied, "if they keep quiet, the stones will cry out." (Luke 19:37-40, NIV)

A soul that has never known peace, joy, love, hope, and forgiveness of sins and then finds all of that in Jesus cannot help but shout to the rooftops, "Hosanna! Blessed is the King who comes in the name of the Lord!" This is the discovery of salvation. Jesus came to save these very ones—the damaged, crying, desperate souls—those hopeless ones who have never seen light, have never experienced true life, meaning, or significance. They cry out because they cannot help it. "Freedom! Hope! Life! Forgiveness! Oh, the tender, compassionate love of Jesus!" He came to save, and save He does.

~ ~ ~

God, shake us. Remind us of the overwhelming joy we had when you first saved us. Take us back to those days when we ran with glee and shouted with thanksgiving for the great salvation you lavished on us when we were dead in our trespasses and sins. Take away our judging hearts for Muslim refugees and migrants. Your soul weeps for them. May our souls weep for them too. And when they call out to you for salvation, may we rejoice exceedingly for the priceless treasure they have found. Help us to understand that a great movement of God is happening today for the Muslim world. You are dispersing them among the nations so that they might be saved, so that they may shout forth the name Jesus! Jesus! Jesus! Plow up our stony hearts. Turn us away from our selfish and provincial interests into the larger area where you are mightily at work drawing every nation to yourself. In Jesus name, Amen.

~ ~ ~

After having encountered and helped many refugees, there is one thing that has been true of nearly all of them I have met. Almost without exception they have not failed to show gratitude and respect for the help they have received from me. Far and away, almost all of these refugees were Muslim. It is quintessentially un-Christian to be without compassion for people in such desperate straits, who did not choose their plight in life or ask to be born into a worldview or into a country that deprives them of all the good blessings we so take for granted.

I have often asked this question to American fathers: "What would you do if you were in their situation? What would you do as a father if you were overwhelmed by catastrophe, your house was being bombed, and you knew that if you did not flee, your daughter and wife would be raped and taken as sex slaves and your sons would be executed?" There is not a father or mother who would not do everything possible to protect and save their family. How in the world can we look into the words of our Holy Book and think for a second that God would not care, or that He would be indifferent to their plight?

THE MAN FROM ALEPPO

I will never forget that day while working in a refugee camp on the Macedonia-Serbia border. Toward the end of the day, as darkness was approaching, I noticed a man around thirty following me. Everywhere I went, I would look up and there he was intently watching me. Just before I left the camp that night, the man approached and embraced me. In broken English he smiled and said, "I am from Aleppo. Thank you for helping us."

The man from Aleppo, an ancient city which has been the epicenter of the cruelest, most devastating and horrific fighting in Syria, saw Jesus for the first time in his life. He saw Jesus through the kind actions and gentle words of all of those Christians who went day in and day out to help this man and to all those exiles of war. To the man from Aleppo, who most likely lost family members and every possession he owned, we represented the goodness, kindness, and compassion his scarred and crying soul desperately craved.

The man from Aleppo represents millions of others devastated by war and calamity, who stand quietly and timidly by, watching our every move, listening to our every word, observing our every action. Absolute fear and desperation is something few of us have ever known. Gripped in the clutches of chaos, the refugees are helplessly and frantically searching for loved ones, desperately calling out for their missing children, being pushed by crowds of people, being herded onto trains going to who knows where, forced into fenced camps, pushing elderly parents and grandparents in wheelchairs through thick mud, and enduring freezing temperatures. These are just some of the hardships they experience. And all the while they are enduring these adversities, they are dealing with the trauma of seeing family and friends being murdered, their homes being razed, and losing everything.

This is why Christians must be there for them. We are the living, active representatives of Jesus in the world. We are the ones who have come to understand the goodness and kindness of God. We are the ones who can bring them hope and comfort when all hope is gone. We are the ones who have been transformed by the saving power of the gospel and who know the promises of God. We are the ones in whom they will see the Jesus of the Bible and feel His nearness and love. Without us, they will know none of this. Without us, they will never experience any answers to their lifelong questions of why it all happened. Without our sacrificial acts of kindness and words of eternal life, they will never ever know the God who sent His Son to save them.

In every catastrophe that God brings, His loving arms are out-stretched and ready to receive all of those who run to Him. But how can they run to Him unless we are there to tell them who He is? "A bruised reed he will not break, and a faintly burning wick he will not quench" (Is. 42:3, ESV).

"As a father shows compassion to his children, so the LORD shows compassion to those who fear him. For he knows our frame; he remembers that we are dust" (Ps. 103:13-14, ESV).

THE MAN FROM MOSUL

In each crisis I've encountered—from Kosovo to Syria to Northern Iraq—I have felt compelled to write about the lives of refugees, of those our teams have personally encountered and those hidden from sight who never appeared but were nonetheless there. Some of us felt helpless in the face of such trauma and suffering. For others, seeing the refugees living through such a catastrophe was a reminder of our own vulnerabilities when faced by impossible circumstances. We would go to help others, but sometimes found ourselves in a reverse role of being the helpless ones. It is likely what God had in mind for us all along.

In Iraq, we were in the midst of a world altogether different than our own. And in that world, human suffering in its humblest and cruelest forms were seen, smelled and felt. We got as close as humanly possible to the war in Mosul, and the places where families have experienced wave after wave of violence, death, suffering and things unimaginable to our senses. It was right where we wanted to be. We stepped into the danger and momentarily into the never-ending fears felt by mothers and little children who clung to our medical staff if only for a few moments of reprieve from their unimaginable lives.

The most touching moment for me occurred on the last day of our trip. We were in a village in East Mosul doing food and water distribution and later a medical clinic in the home of an Iraqi military commander. Word went out to the community that a team had come to provide medical care. Within a short period of time, the room was filled with covered Muslim mothers with their small children. One after another, as they had done before, our medical personnel treated each patient as best they could.

During this time, I was outside talking to some of the men of Mosul. One of the community leaders would hardly leave my side. We communicated as best we could in the few words he knew in English. He had once been a taxi driver in Baghdad. We laughed with one another, and though we had never met before and had come from completely different backgrounds, we formed a bond. As we stood next to the door where just inside was the room overflowing with Iraqi women and children, he looked at me and pointed to his face, just under his eye. "Pain," he said. Since we were doing a clinic I immediately thought he was describing a physical pain he was suffering somewhere around his eye. Then the tears began to trickle down his face, and he put his palms together and said, "Pray." So, with him, in a childlike manner I put my hands together, bowed my head, and prayed that God would pity and pour out His mercy on the broken people gathered in the living room just feet from us and for the inhabitants of the great city of Mosul.

The man from Mosul wanted me to see his pain for his people and then asked me to pray for them. It was as if Jesus himself were standing there weeping over the city, beseeching his disciples to pray for the peace of Mosul. This Muslim man expressed better than I could the heart of God for a people so near and dear to him. God once said of these same people thousands of years ago, "Should I not pity Nineveh, that great city in which there are more than 120,000 [children] who do not know their right hand from their left?" (Jonah 4:11, ESV).

IS ANYONE THERE?

Recently, during a United Nations meeting on human rights in North Korea, a defector by the name of Ji Hyeon-A spoke about her tragic experiences at the hands of North Korean authorities after being repatriated three times from China. After her third repatriation, she was forced to abort her three-month-old child. She spoke of the horrors pregnant women endure: "Pregnant women were forced into harsh labor all day. . . . At night, we heard pregnant mothers screaming and babies died without ever being able to see their mothers."[1]

Here is a poem Ji Hyeon-A wrote while enduring indescribable horrors in North Korea, and shared at the UN meeting:

> I am scared, is anyone there? I'm here in hell, is anyone there? I scream and yell but no one opens the door. Is anyone there? Please listen to our moans and listen to our pain. Is anyone there? People are dying, my friend is dying. I call out again and again, but why don't you answer. Is anyone there?[2]

Indifference to the suffering of people is not difficult to attain. It only takes one action: to turn our eyes away from the very objects of God's deepest love and pity. But just as easy as it is to become cold by the act of looking away, God can fill our hearts with the sunshine of His love for others by simply turning our heads and looking into the eyes of those we find unpleasant.

~ ~ ~

Oh, Lord, we simply will never know you until we peer into the sufferings of the world around us. It is easy to want to know you in the power of your resurrection, but the deep knowledge of God cannot come until we enter in to the fellowship of your sufferings. Turn our eyes to gaze upon the very objects of your passion. May we learn to loathe the cynical expressions of our fallen nature that despise those who are not like us. Remind us that, but for the grace of God, we would be no different. We, too, were once far from you and in need of your pity just like them. Oh, thank you that you saved us. Now, Lord, Jehovah-Shammah, the God who is there, save them. In Jesus name, Amen.

~ ~ ~

CHALLENGING THE STATUS QUO

Whether we are discussing cross-cultural missions or local outreach, we are called to be salt and light wherever God places us. None of us need a special label or even a specific gifting before we are released to do the work of God in the world. The status quo says that you are exempt from doing certain types of ministry if you do not have the title, the gift, or the calling. How often do we hear expressions such as, "I could never do what you are doing" or "God didn't call me to do that" or even "I don't have that particular gift." Often, these are all convenient ways of exempting ourselves from sharing with others and engaging real human need around us.

While each of us have received assigned gifts from the Holy Spirit, that does not mean we can claim exemption from other services. Just because you or I don't have the gift of evangelism does that mean we don't have to evangelize? If you or I don't have the gift of hospitality, does that somehow mean we don't have to show hospitality? This false view of ministry has hindered the progress of the gospel and kept the church from caring for the needs of others as it should. It is the Pareto principle, also known as the law of the vital few, which says that roughly 80 percent of the effects comes from 20 percent of the causes. Basically, this 80/20 rule says that about 80 percent of the world benefits from the 20 percent who do most of the work.[3] But as the Body of Christ, every member plays an essential role in the function of the body, even when members practice certain services where they are not specially gifted in those areas.

In the case of global catastrophes, there isn't a large pool of gifted people to select from to do the hard and dangerous work that needs to be done. This is where we move in to the 99.5/0.5 rule where possibly only around 0.5 percent of Christians are doing the cross-cultural work of the 99.5 percent. Whether or not these workers can do the job is of little importance. What is important is the job needs to be done, and you may be the only one there to do it. In those instances, when we yield ourselves to God, He supernaturally enables us to do what we thought was not possible.

Though many churches and mission organizations have tailored their approach to doing outreach and ministry in certain ways, this does not mean they are incapable of reorienting themselves as demands change. Catastrophes will continue to increase, affecting both local and global outreach efforts, and changes need to be made to prepare for how and when Christians respond regardless of whether or not we think we are called to do so.

HOW WE MOVE FORWARD

How we move forward from here is of great importance. We have looked at the role of catastrophe from the beginning of time, through the present, and into the future. Catastrophes are on the rise and will continue to gain in intensity and severity until the King of kings and Lord of lords sets up His kingdom on earth. The biblical blueprint is clear.

If the Father's goal is to fill the earth with His glory through the salvation of all nations, which He will one day award to Jesus as His inheritance, then nothing should distract or hinder us from completing this work of God in His world. This is our last-days call. Our task is to deliver to Christ the remaining unreached peoples of the earth, but we must understand that these remaining groups will come at a steep price. Satan will fight us with all the powers of darkness to deny Jesus the prize of all nations, the inheritance He will receive and share with us in His kingdom.

This means that access to many of the unreached peoples of the world will most certainly occur by way of catastrophe, which God will send to loosen the grip Satan has over them. Many of the normal or traditional ways we've used to gain access and minister among them is rapidly becoming a thing of the past. We must be prepared in these new times and boldly take necessary steps to reorganize and modify our methods for dealing with worst-case scenarios. The first step in doing this is to comprehend the urgency of the times. We must move from business as usual, to a rapid response kind of readiness. The nature of catastrophe demands it. While catastrophe brings a sense of urgency, it also involves ever-shifting geopolitical complications as multiple nations are usually involved. According to former Secretary of State Henry Kissinger, geopolitics is "an approach that pays attention to the requirements of equilibrium."[4] This requirement of equilibrium is another step and cannot be detached from a global missions strategy of today. We must be more knowledgeable regarding the rise and fall of governments and the geographic and political changes they bring. We also need to be in the business of opportunity forecasting. This is when you analyze current geopolitical standings against the global movements of God so that you can better predict what may happen in crisis prone areas of the world where opportunities may open up to spread the gospel. The quantum jump in technology has made global communication so much faster and easier. Today the world has become a virtual office in which we can all meet at any place and any time. The necessity of having people working full-time in a physical office from nine to five is becoming obsolete. In world missions this means one person easily can give a percentage of his or her time to a network of organizations. It is an efficient and effective model that will streamline response efforts. Multiple entities gain from the experience or expertise of the one individual who may spend only 10 percent of a work week filling a particular role. This resource sharing through virtual offices increases readiness and keeps organizations from becoming too costly, cumbersome, and top heavy.

CATASTROPHE: THE NEW MISSION PARADIGM

Catastrophe clearly has become the landscape of God's redemptive mission on earth.

Catastrophe has become the new normal. Destructive storms, prolonged droughts, massive floods, increased wildfires, heat waves, violent volcanoes and more are regular occurrences today. The sharp increase in global terrorism, sectarian violence, jihadist attacks, regional wars, and ethnic conflicts correspondingly are spiraling out of control on a global scale. None of these things are static. They are increasing in frequency and intensity and are directly impacting all of us.

Catastrophes are like a high and hazardous mountain we must climb to reach those who remain in the iron grip of antichristian regimes and religions, especially Islam. The higher we climb the slopes and through the perilous storms of catastrophe, the more difficult and dangerous the task, but the sweeter the prize.

As we ascend the mountain, each step we take will get tougher and tougher. There will be little reprieve as terrorism, sectarian violence, war, and natural and environmental disasters will strike with greater magnitude and intensity. To ascend to the top, we will need to be refitted with the proper tools and training for the faith and endurance required.

The steady global events of the past allowed for a slower evangelistic approach. When politics were more constant, mission organizations could take longer to plan the movement in and out of targeted areas. That has all given way to the avalanche of rapid-fire calamitous events occurring almost daily. The Bible said all of this would happen as the end draws near. Jesus' disciples specifically asked Him what would be "the sign of your coming, and the end of the age?" (Matt. 24:3) Jesus replied:

> See that no one leads you astray. For many will come in my name, saying, 'I am the Christ,' and they will lead many astray. And you will hear of wars and rumors of wars. See that you are not alarmed, for this must take place, but the end is not yet. For nation will rise against nation, and kingdom against kingdom, and there will be famines and earthquakes in various places. All these are but the beginning of the birth pains. (Matthew 24:4-8)

Jesus' reference to a simultaneous drastic rise of both natural and man-made disasters was not cryptic. He clearly said that, not just one, but both must occur at the same time before the end would come. The phenomena we see today is exactly this. It is not one or the other; it is clearly both.

This is not lost on some scientists who are seeing a connection between natural catastrophes and wars. Scientists say they have proved that "heatwaves, droughts and other severe weather events are increasing the risk of wars breaking out across the world."[5] Whether or not climate change is what is causing the increase of natural disasters that are leading to armed, ethnic conflict, is a matter of debate and is not relevant here. What is relevant is that even secular scientists recognize the causal relationship between man-made wars, ethnic conflicts, and natural or environmental disasters. This correlation was specifically predicted by Jesus.

If we are to move forward and make gospel advances onto this new landscape, the first step in this paradigm shift will require accepting both the cataclysmic realities around us, and the application of faith in what we see in the words of Scripture. God is fully unveiling to us the central role catastrophe has played in His plan for the nations and how catastrophe will be the focal mechanism for completing that task in the last days.

The great philosophical question "Why does God allow suffering" is not only asked by the "civilized" and educated. It is asked by all who cannot find relief or answers in their greatest suffering. I can tell you this because I know. I've seen it and experienced it many times. A kind act, a caring smile and words of comfort from the child of God to a hurting soul revives his hope in God. There is nothing complex to contemplate about our response. It is not like trying to strike up a conversation with an agnostic in a university classroom. When people are humiliated, alone and defeated there is only one thing they want, and that is to be comforted. And their greatest comfort can only come from us in whom the One who is called Comforter resides.

—SYRIAN REFUGEE CRISIS, PERSONAL JOURNAL, FEBRUARY 29, 2016

13

A MISSIONARY FOR THE TIMES

And most of the brothers, having become confident in the Lord by my imprisonment,
are much more bold to speak the word without fear.

—PHIL. 1:14

CULTIVATING A NEW BREED OF CHRISTIAN AND MISSIONARY
We are living in new times, and these new times require us to confront how we operate as Christ's witness in the world. As His disciples, we should always be learners in both the secular and the spiritual arenas since God operates in both. However, in much of Western evangelicalism today, it is popular to surround ourselves with everything "Christian." How often do we hear a brother or sister talking about the huge blessing of finding a house in a subdivision, surrounded by Christian neighbors? As evangelicals, we are becoming more and more sectarian in where we live, who we associate with, and even who we do business with. Everywhere we go, we see believers seeking their fortunes and then building their fortresses to keep out those with whom they do not agree, or who make them feel uncomfortable. Western evangelicalism is quickly losing its global influence because it is turning inward. If Western Christians are going to make the kind of positive and eternal impact necessary to meet the new and growing challenges

and opportunities we face, it is imperative that we reverse this trend.

Lost also in this generation is the value of personal sacrifice. Sadly, we are swiftly becoming a narcissistic, comfort-focused people, more interested in the superficial church show experience, than we are in our sacrificial service to the lost. As global dangers and threats increase, we need a special breed of Christ-ones who are willing to sacrifice the promises of worldly comfort, security, and personal recognition for the sake of the call of God for the nations. But we don't have to look back very far to find the examples we need. I (Nathan) have been blessed to marry into a missionary family. My mother and father-in-law left for the jungles of Brazil in the early 1950s. Their stories of living and working among one of the most primitive, endo-cannibalistic people groups in Brazil are epic. They faced death, sickness, disease, warfare, hardship, deprivation, isolation, and discouragement as a normal part of their Christian experience for nearly forty years.

Often, in those days, missionaries would take their caskets with them on the boats because they knew they may never come home. When they kissed their aging parents goodbye, they knew they would probably never see them again in this life. Missionary service was the ultimate sacrifice that meant giving up everything for their Savior. When life got tough, there was no out. The only option available to them was to cry out in desperation to the God of all comfort who supports us in all of our afflictions.

We are honored to know others who are of this same caliber—men and women of whom this world is not worthy. But they are a rare and dying breed. Oh, to God if we could have more of them! Who will take their place? Who among this generation will stand up and say, I don't care what this world promises me. It means nothing. I want only to be used by God. I want only to be his willing and obedient instrument to rescue the perishing. I will give my all for Him and I don't care what happens to me. I rest myself in the loving and secure hands of my Savior.

This world will only be reached by such saints. The easier places are already taken. There remain only the very hard and dangerous places.

Those prized people of God living in these locations will come to know Jesus only by those willing to give up everything for their salvation. To walk this way is to emulate the response of the first-century believers and those brave, faithful servants who followed their example, and who've stood on their shoulders through the centuries. Who today will stand with them?

FEARLESS IN THE FACE OF CATASTROPHE

Sadly, much of missions and evangelism today is marked by fear. One day I was driving to a consultation in Atlanta. On my way, I saw a billboard with an advertisement that said, "Safety Is Our Motto." I immediately wondered if what I was reading was the purpose statement of a modern-day missionary sending organization. Many well-known mission agencies today spend an inordinate amount of time and energy to train missionaries in how to keep safe and inconspicuous. I would venture to say that more focus is given to keeping the missionary safe and secure than there is in training them to live by faith, and to take risks that may require them giving their lives for the people they've been sent to serve.

This sends a disturbing message of fear and self-preservation to the very nationals that missionaries have gone to reach. Rather than communicating to them the importance of boldly living by faith and being willing to risk their lives and safety for the progress of the gospel, it tells them that in the face of being discovered, they need to hide or flee. Imagine the kind of Christian that breeds? Does this mean the missionary should be careless and unwise and risk the safety and security of others? No. What it means is that we live by another standard, one that we find in the Bible. It means we live by faith in the power of God, and that by living this way, God will perform miracles exceedingly, abundantly above anything we could ever ask or think.

There is no doubt that many young Muslim men are drawn to radical jihadist groups because of the risk it offers. Men want to be challenged to do hard and dangerous things. Could it be that one of the biggest reasons we don't see more young people going into missions today is because they are not being challenged on this level? We've emasculated the mission of God by trying to recruit people by selling them a package that says the task is palatable, short-term, and fun, rather than telling them the truth. What if we just put it out there like it really is. What if we said this: We are making a call for a specialized group of men and women to participate in something bigger and greater than anything they have ever experienced or known in their lives. We are selecting an elite group to carry the most important message the world has ever known to the last remaining groups of people in the world before Jesus returns. But before you reply, you must understand what you are getting yourself into and the probable dangers you will face. If you would so choose to be among this select group, you should consider the following:

- You will be persecuted for the name of Jesus Christ.

- Your lifestyle will be completely altered, and where you live may never become home.

- You will experience long periods of isolation and discouragement.

- You may never see in this life the fruit of your labors.

- Because of the arduous work entailed, most of the time you will be exhausted.

- Your family and children will suffer and go without most things others enjoy.

- You will likely be harassed physically.

- You may be taken hostage.

- You may lose your life.

The rewards for your service in this life are minimal, but the prize you will receive in the next life will be beyond comprehension. But the greatest reward you will receive will be the knowledge that you have volunteered yourself to enter in to the highest and most honorable service of the King of kings and Lord of lords, and the pleasure you will bring to Him for doing so.

We need this new breed of Christian worker, and we need this new message to recruit them for this new, global mission paradigm. The bar for serving is as high as it has ever been, and the need for those willing to go is as great as we've seen. The size of the vision and the faith of those needing to go must fit the size of the enormous task this generation has been given. In light of what is presently before us, with the rise of catastrophes and what is to come, the time has arrived for us to clearly communicate that we can have nothing less in this final push for the nations.

INTENTIONALLY GOING TO THE HARD PLACES

This new breed of Christian worker must be willing to go and stay in the hard places. The term previously used for these locations was "creative access" countries. This term should be upgraded to "dangerous access." This new catchword better and more honestly clarifies the risks and the level of difficulty in penetrating these last frontiers. Many of the catastrophes and much of the civil unrest occurring in the world are taking place in some of the most dangerous access countries, such as Iran, Iraq, Syria, Afghanistan, Libya, Yemen, North Korea, Pakistan, and Turkey. But entrance to these disaster hotspots is not impossible.

Catastrophes are forcing the doors open. Access and freedom to work in areas affected by disaster, or in the regions where refugees are fleeing to, are often made possible because of the chaos brought on by war and natural disasters. Governments and local authorities are often destabilized and unable to cope with the overwhelming damage and flood of humanity. Time and resources are diverted from normal operations to focusing on the pressing needs around them. The best friend of the gospel is a country in chaos. Often, when disasters strike, this is the time to run to, not flee from, those places.

We need to be sufficiently prepared and ready to mobilize at the moment these doors open. When entrance is made, that is the time for Christian workers to make a positive impact and to gain credibility in its handling of disasters without compromising the gospel. There are never any guarantees workers will be able to even get into these crisis-prone and affected areas of the world, or to remain there if they do gain entrance, but every effort should be made to do so before, during, and after crises occur. Evangelical mission organizations should be pressing hard on the doors of all difficult and dangerous access countries until a way is made possible for them to enter, most probably when catastrophe strikes. When they enter, they should arrive with:

- competent people who can quickly and intelligently assess and respond to the situation;

- overwhelming humanitarian support for affected people; and

- their feet shod with the preparation of the gospel of peace.

Trails are blazed and new frontiers are forged by those with enormous faith who are willing to take great personal risks and do the hard and dangerous work. There is nothing gained by trying to temper this truth. It is a new time with an old calling for a uniquely willing and prepared generation.

TAKING A STAND FOR THE TRUTH

Soon after I came to faith in Christ, my father, who ran from the Lord for the first fourteen years of my life, returned to the Good Shepherd. During those years in the wilderness, God never let my father forget the joy he once knew when he walked in the fresh, green paths of righteousness. Every time Dad tried to go his own way, the Lord would withhold any satisfaction or peace of mind.

Finally, one day when my dad was driving home from work to our little town in southern Indiana, God took hold of him in a way that completely revolutionized his life. The experience he encountered so radically shook him that he never again denied God his total devotion until the day he died. That evening, my father was speeding down rural Highway 67, trying to get home as fast as he could to miss the worst of what has been called the Great Blizzard of 1978, also called the White Hurricane that struck the Ohio Valley. It was a natural disaster—a Category 5 storm that, over two days, dumped two feet of snow with fierce wind gusts of up to forty-five miles an hour. It was called the storm of the century.

Without warning, Dad's car went into a spin. It spun three times, and in that space of time his life flashed before his eyes. By the end of the second rotation, according to my father, his heart was right with God. He went into the spin with a selfish, rebellious heart and when it ended moments later, he came out with a heart as clean and pure as the shimmering white snow that engulfed him.

From that day forward, my dad made it his aim to make up for his lost years by teaching me and his other children still at home the incomprehensible and indescribable value of the cross of Jesus Christ. My dad—my discipler and mentor—repeatedly said to me, "Nathan, never forget the cross. Never forget what Jesus did for you." I have made it my own aim to honor my earthly and heavenly Father's request to do this very thing.

While tactics, strategies and methods change to adapt our message to fit the context of the times, we have but one message for the world. It is the message of the cross of Jesus Christ. The apostle Paul said to the Corinthian believers, "For I decided to know nothing among you except Jesus Christ and Him crucified" (1 Cor. 2:2, ESV). This decision Paul made was more narrowly defined when he told the believers in Rome, "and thus I make it my ambition to preach the gospel, not where Christ has already been named, lest I build on someone else's foundation" (Rom. 15:20, ESV).

The message that Jesus Christ, the promised Deliverer—the very Son of God—came into the world to die on a cross, be buried, and rise again from the dead to save sinners, is the one and only message of hope and life we have been given to share to the world. Anything or anyone that takes away from this central truth, takes away the one and only message able to restore a lost soul to God, and, thus destroys its power to regenerate the heart of man.

This is the truth on which we must take our stand in the last days. In our culture of political correctness, in which so many young people have grown up, many are falling away from the faith and not holding to or even understanding the anchor of the cross. Popular positions on migration, refugees, and humanitarian assistance, are adopted by Christians and fiercely defended, but few are standing for the uniquely Christian message of the gospel of the cross and resurrection of Jesus Christ.

What eternal good does it do to a migrant or refugee if our work is only to give them food, water, clothing, and shelter? How are we fulfilling our God-given mandate from Jesus to a migrant or refugee if all we offer to them are smiles, kindness, and solidarity? Even the godless do the same. If our acts of grace and kindness are not tied to the message of the cross, we have done them no service of eternal good. Unless we give them the bread of life, they will perish in their sins. It may make us feel good to contribute to the needs of the poor and needy, but unless we offer living water to their withered souls, they have gained nothing. And possibly they have lost the only opportunity they may have ever had to encounter a Christian and hear the story of salvation in Jesus Christ.

If the cries of this generation and Christian leaders in the West for open borders and more refugees is not met with a commitment to deliver the gospel when they arrive on our shores, then the efforts are hardly more than political activism. To Christians who are opposed to refugees at all, we must point out that just as much as we are not called to be political activists, neither are we to be sectarianists who elevate national interests above people's souls. For evangelicals, our highest cause—the rallying cry for which we should be willing to give our lives—is the saving power of the cross for all people.

In today's raging debate about migrants and refugees, both sides are missing what should be at the center of our discussion. This should not be about taking political or even humanitarian sides. For Christians, especially evangelicals, the refugee issue should be about eternal souls and what God has done and is doing to save them through us. If the gospel message is not central to our position on migrants and refugees, we are doomed to an endless debate about the virtues or the threats to our societies. Neither side is going to prevail, and may, in fact, only serve to further divide the church if we persist in pushing views that are devoid of the cross. But if we are unified in the belief that all people need Jesus Christ and that this message must be shared with them, then we are in lockstep with God's foremost command and concern given to each of us. "We must have the courage to articulate a gospel-centered approach to this issue. It is our duty to view immigrants not as problems to solve but as people for whom Jesus died. Without a biblical lens, we may come to view immigrants as a threat and an invasion, rather than as a missional opportunity. In doing so, we lose credibility with our immigrant neighbors when, while proclaiming Christ's love to them, we also communicate (intentionally or otherwise) that we dislike them and wish they were not part of our communities."[1]

IT WILL BE WORTH IT ALL

If it is true

- that from the beginning of time God has had a plan and a consistent strategy to one day save and restore His creation by revealing His love and grace to humanity through the death and resurrection of His Son;

- that God gave to Israel and then the church His command to spread His message of salvation to the ends of the earth;

- that throughout the narrative of Scripture God has consistently orchestrated catastrophe in order to scatter people as exiles and refugees to fill the earth with His glory in the salvation of all nations;

- that God scatters the nations directly into the path of His people in order for them to be exposed to the gospel;

- that we are living in the last days, and because of this, God is exponentially stepping up His activity of giving unreached peoples access to the truth of God's Word through disaster before His return;

- that we might be the last, privileged generation entrusted with His salvation message to preach to the last generation of people who will hear before the return of Jesus;

- that the remaining unreached peoples, held in the clutches of antiChristian empires of the earth may very well be released to hear the words of eternal life as a result of some kind of man-made or natural disaster;

- that Jesus handed to us the unspeakable privilege of delivering the nations to Jesus as His longed for and much deserved inheritance;

- that He waits for us to finish the task He gave us to hand the nations to Him;

- that He will one day share this inheritance of the nations with us when He rules the world with righteousness and justice;

. . . then what manner of people ought we to be?

If we understood that we play a vital and irreplaceable role in all of these things, then shouldn't it change us? But to be changed, we must understand that the cost involves loving those who hate us. They are enemies of the cross, but God wants them to embrace the cross, that they may be made His friends and ours. We, too, were once hostile to God and enemies of His, but He saved us (see Rom. 5:10). And as God redeemed us, His utmost desire is to do the same for the whole world:

> For God was pleased to have all his fullness dwell in him and through
> him to reconcile to himself all things, whether things on earth or

things in heaven, by making peace through his blood, shed on the cross. (Colossians 1:19-20, NIV)

Dietrich Bonhoeffer said,

Words and thoughts are not enough. Doing good involves all the things of daily life. 'If your enemies are hungry, feed them; if they are thirsty, give them something to drink' (Romans 12:20). In the same ways that brothers and sisters stand by each other in times of need, bind up each other's wounds, ease each other's pain, love of the enemy should do good to the enemy. Where in the world is there greater need, where are deeper wounds and pain than those of our enemies? Where is doing good more necessary and more blessed than for our enemies?

CONCLUSION

The stunning beauty of God's interaction with man in the narrative of history has been most clearly seen in catastrophe. No great story is ever told without it. Tragedy is what gives the story the happiest and most satisfying ending possible. F. Scott Fitzgerald wrote, "Show me a hero and I'll write you a tragedy." All tragedies have a hero, and in the human story of calamity, a hero is given.

In epic, narrative style Paul concludes:

But when the fullness of time had come, God sent forth His Son, born of woman, born under the law, to redeem those who were under the law, so that we might receive adoption as sons. (Galatians 4:4-5, ESV)

In him we have redemption through his blood, the forgiveness of our trespasses, according to the riches of his grace, which he lavished upon us, in all wisdom and insight making known to us the mystery of his will, according to his purpose, which he set forth in Christ as a plan for the fullness of time, to unite all things in him, things in heaven and things on earth. (Ephesians 1:7-10, ESV)

The catastrophes of history have not been meaningless. God's plan was that in the fullness of time, He would reveal the hero of the story who would make sense of all the suffering mankind has endured throughout the ages. From the chaos is revealed a mystery of unimaginable grace from God to His creation. More than has ever been given out, by way of indescribable human suffering, God has taken upon Himself in the person of His Son. The promised Deliverer finally came, and His tragedy was greater than any catastrophe to ever befall mankind, for God made "him who knew no sin to be sin for us, so that we might become the righteousness of God" (2 Cor. 5:21, NIV).

Before the first human disaster ever struck, God determined that He Himself would bear all of the suffering of man's failures on Himself when He would come and die on a wooden cross. If we are tempted to think it has been unfair that God would orchestrate catastrophe in human affairs, can we still remain uncertain in light of this truth?

We know the story's end. There we are with Him on that day, alongside a countless sea of heavenly citizens from every tribe, language, people and nation with our own stories of salvation written from the crucible of disaster. And there He stands—the epitome of catastrophe, sacrificed for our redemption, a Lamb in the midst of the throne, slain before the foundation of the world. He receives us, His prize, and we sing the song of redemption.

Out of the ashes of catastrophe, over the millennia of the ages, a light has dawned, and we have yet to witness its glorious ending. It all comes down to love—not our love for God, but God's love for us. The plan was never for the purpose of condemning. It was always to redeem. If there was ever a victim in the story, it was not man, but God. But instead of becoming the martyr of the story, He became the hero and we have made ourselves the martyr. This is the mystery of catastrophe.

Notes

CHAPTER 2: HIS WAY IS IN THE WHIRLWIND

1. Melissa Petruzzello, "Playing with Wildfire: 5 Amazing Adaptations of Pyrophytic Plants," *Encylopaedia Britannica*, https://www.britannica.com/list/5-amazing-adaptations-of-pyrophytic-plants.

CHAPTER 3: THE MYSTERY OF CATASTROPHE

1. Coen Vonk, "Mysteries of Ancient Greece," *Sunrise* magazine, Theosophical University Press, 2005, http://www.theosociety.org/pasadena/sunrise/54-04-5/me-vonk.htm.
2. Matthew Soerens and Daniel Darling, "The Gospel and Immigration," *Gospel Coalition*, MAY 1, 2012, https://www.thegospelcoalition.org/article/the-gospel-and-immigration/.
3. Peter Yeung, "Refugee crisis: Record 65 million people forced to flee homes, UN says," *Independent*, June 20, 2016, http://www.independent.co.uk/news/world/europe/refugee-crisis-migrants-world-day-un-a7090986.html.

CHAPTER 4: PRESENT-DAY EXAMPLES

1. "Albania timeline," BBC News, January 24, 2012, http://news.bbc.co.uk/2/hi/europe/country_profiles/1004984.stm.
2. "Quick facts: What you need to know about the Syria crisis," Mercy Corps, July 19, 2018, https://www.mercycorps.org/articles/iraq-jordan-lebanon-syria-turkey/quick-facts-what-you-need-know-about-syria-crisis.
3. "Quick facts: What you need to know about the Syria crisis," Mercy Corps, July 19, 2018, https://www.mercycorps.org/articles/iraq-jordan-lebanon-syria-turkey/quick-facts-what-you-need-know-about-syria-crisis.
4. Anne Barnard, "Death Toll from War in Syria Now 470,000, Group Finds," *New York Times*, February 11, 2016, https://www.nytimes.com/2016/02/12/world/middleeast/death-toll-from-war-in-syria-now-470000-group-finds.html.
5. "The world's 5 biggest refugee crises," Mercy Corps, July 5, 2018, https://www.mercycorps.org/articles/afghanistan-nigeria-somalia-south-sudan-syria/worlds-5-biggest-refugee-crises.
6. Nick Cumming-Bruce and Rick Gladstone, "U.N. Says 5,000 Syrians a Day Are Now Fleeing War," *New York Times*, February 8, 2013, http://www.nytimes.com/2013/02/09/world/middleeast/syria-refugees.html.
7. Ruadhán Mac Cormaic, "Year when Europe opened its doors to refugees," *Irish Times*, December 28, 2015, https://www.irishtimes.com/news/world/europe/year-when-europe-opened-its-doors-to-refugees-1.2478737.

CHAPTER 5: THE BIG PICTURE OF CATASTROPHE

1. http://www.dictionary.com/browse/strategy?s=t.
2. "Haiti," Operation World, 2018, http://www.operationworld.org/country/hait/owtext.html.
3. Kari Huus, "Haiti awash in Christian aid, evangelism," MSNBC, February 9, 2009, http://www.nbcnews.com/id/35262608/ns/world_news-haiti/t/haiti-awash-christian-aid-evangelism/#.WoqZ5mXHFlI.
4. "Has Everyone Heard?" Joshua Project, https://joshuaproject.net/resources/articles/has_everyone_heard.
5. "What is the 10/40 Window?" Joshua Project, https://joshuaproject.net/resources/articles/10_40_window.
6. "10/40 Window: Do you need to be stirred to action?" Southern Nazarene University, https://home.snu.edu/~hculbert/1040.htm.
7. David Russell Schilling, "Knowledge Doubling Every 12 Months, Soon to be Every 12 Hours," *Industry Tap*, April 19, 2013, http://www.industrytap.com/knowledge-doubling-every-12-months-soon-to-be-every-12-hours/3950.
8. Ibid.

CHAPTER 6: A WORLD OF CATASTROPHE

1. "The Human Cost of Weather Related Disasters: 1995-2015," Center for Research on the Epidemiology of Disasters, https://www.unisdr.org/2015/docs/climatechange/COP21_WeatherDisastersReport_2015_FINAL.pdf.
2. Ibid.
3. Tom Miles, "Weather disasters occur almost daily, becoming more frequent: U.N." Reuters, November 23, 2015, https://www.reuters.com/article/us-climatechange-disasters/weather-disasters-occur-almost-daily-becoming-more-frequent-u-n-idUSKBN0TC1EG20151123.
4. "U.S. Billion-Dollar Weather & Climate Disasters 1980-2018," National Centers for Environmental Information, https://www.ncdc.noaa.gov/billions/events.pdf.
5. Chris Mooney and Brady Dennis, "Extreme hurricanes and wildfires made 2017 the most costly U.S. disaster year on record," *Washington Post*, January 8, 2018, https://www.washingtonpost.com/news/energy-environment/wp/2018/01/08/hurricanes-wildfires-made-2017-the-most-costly-u-s-disaster-year-on-record/?utm_term=.fcf9dcdaf03d.
6. "Weather-related disasters are increasing," *Economist*, August 29, 2017, https://www.economist.com/graphic-detail/2017/08/29/weather-related-disasters-are-increasing.
7. Jerry Z. Muller, "Us and Them," Foreign Affairs, March/April 2008, https://www.foreignaffairs.com/articles/europe/2008-03-02/us-and-them.
8. "List of ongoing armed conflicts," Wikipedia, updated August 4, 2018, https://en.wikipedia.org/wiki/List_of_ongoing_armed_conflicts.
9. Glenn J. Voelz, *Rise of iWar: Identity, Information, and the Individualization of Modern Warfare* (New York: Skyhorse Publishing, 2018).
10. "Guide to the Syrian rebels," BBC, December 13, 2013, http://www.bbc.com/news/world-middle-east-24403003.
11. Joe Lauria, "Risking World War III in Syria," *Consortium News*, February 6, 2016, https://consortiumnews.com/2016/02/06/risking-world-war-iii-in-syria/.

CHAPTER 7: THE LAST REICH

1. Cristina Maza, "Christian Persecution And Genocide Is Worse Now Than 'Any Time In History,' Report Says," *Newsweek*, January 4, 2018, http://www.newsweek.com/christian-persecution-genocide-worse-ever-770462.

2. Sarah Eekhoff Zylstra, "The Top 50 Countries Where It's Most Dangerous to Follow Jesus," *Christianity Today*, January 10, 2018, http://www.christianitytoday.com/news/2018/january/top-50-christian-persecution-open-doors-world-watch-list.html.

3. Samuel P. Huntington, *The Clash of Civilizations and the Remaking of World Order* (New York, Simon & Schuster, 1998), 25.

4. Michael Lipka, "Muslims and Islam: Key findings in the U.S. and around the world," August 9, 2017, http://www.pewresearch.org/fact-tank/2017/08/09/muslims-and-islam-key-findings-in-the-u-s-and-around-the-world/.

5. Ibn Ishaq, *The Life of Muhammad*, trans. A. Guillaume (Oxford: Oxford University Press, 2002).

6. Ibn Ishaq, *The Life of Muhammad*, trans. A. Guillaume (Oxford: Oxford University Press, 2002), 464.

7. Quran in Today's English. Clear and Easy to Read. Translated by Talal Itani.

8. Sahih al-Bukhari (Vol. 1, Bk. 8), 387.

9. Robert G. Hoyland, *Seeing Islam As Others Saw It: A Survey and Evaluation of Christian, Jewish and Zoroastrian Writings on Early Islam* (Pennington, NJ: The Darwin Press, Inc. 1997), 554-5.

10. Islam's Awaiting Messiah: "Tafsir Ibn Kathir Surah 9:123 Tafsir.com.

11. Imam al-Waqidi, The Conquest of Persia, al-Tabari reports on Islam's enormous victory at the Battle of Jalula' al-Waqi'ah.

12. Bat Ye'Or, *The Decline of Eastern Christianity Under Islam: From Jihad to Dhimmitude* (Vancouver, BC: Fairleigh Dickinson University Press, 1996), 44.

13. Samuel P. Huntington, The Clash of Civilizations and the Remaking of World Order.

14. R. James Woolsey, testimony before the U.S. Senate Committee on Foreign Relations, November 16, 2005, https://www.foreign.senate.gov/imo/media/doc/WoolseyTestimony051116.pdf.

15. Yousaf Butt, "How Saudi Wahhabism Is the Fountainhead of Islamist Terrorism," *Huffington Post*, January 20, 2015, http://www.huffingtonpost.com/dr-yousaf-butt-/saudi-wahhabism-islam-terrorism_b_6501916.html.

16. Chas Danner, "Report: ISIS Has Recruited as Many as 30,000 Foreigners in the Past Year," *New York Magazine*, September 27, 2015, http://nymag.com/daily/intelligencer/2015/09/isis-has-recruited-as-many-as-30000-foreigners.html.

17. Betsy Cooper, Daniel Cox, Ph.D., Rachel Lienesch, Robert P. Jones, Ph.D., "Exodus: Why Americans are Leaving Religion—and Why They're Unlikely to Come Back," Public Religion Research Institute, September 22, 2016, https://www.prri.org/research/prri-rns-poll-nones-atheist-leaving-religion/.

18. Tertullian, *Apologeticus*, Chapter 50 s.13.

19. Philip Jenkins, *Images of Terror: What We Can and Can't Know about Terrorism* (Piscataway, NJ: Aldine Transaction, 2003).

CHAPTER 8: THE SPIRIT OF ANTICHRIST

1. Translation by Muhammad Sarwar.

2. Tafsir Ibn Kathir, abridged by Shaykh Safiur-Rahman Al-Mubarakpuri, et al. Maktaba Dar-us-Salam—Second Edition, 2003] volume 4, 377.

3. "The World's Muslims: Unity and Diversity: Chapter 3: Articles of Faith," Pew Research Center, August 9, 2012, http://www.pewforum.org/2012/08/09/the-worlds-muslims-unity-and-diversity-3-articles-of-faith/#end-times.

4. "Dabiq: Why is Syrian town so important for IS?" BBC, October 4, 2016, https://www.bbc.com/news/world-middle-east-30083303.

5. Nour Malas, "Ancient Prophecies Motivate Islamic State Militants," *Wall Street Journal*, November 18, 2014, https://www.wsj.com/articles/ancient-prophecies-motivate-islamic-state-militants-1416357441.

6. *Wall Street Journal*, "Ancient Prophecies Motivate Islamic State Militants: Battlefield Strategies Driven by 1,400-year-old Apocalyptic Ideas" November 18, 2014.

7. President Erdoğan speaking at the AK Party's Rize Provincial Congress, November 18, 2017, https://www.tccb.gov.tr/en/news/542/87380/our-nation-assigned-us-the-duty-of-establishing-a-greater-and-stronger-turkey.

8. Ahmad, *al-Musnad* 14:331 #18859; al-Hakim, al-Mustadrak 4:421-422; al-Tabarani, al-Mu`jam al-Kabir 2:38 #1216; Bukhari, al-Tarikh al-Kabir 2:81 and al-Saghir 1:306; Suyuti, al-Jami` al-Saghir.

9. Ibn Kathir, *Signs Before the Day of Judgement* (Ellicott City, MD, Dar Al Taqwa, Ltd.), 8.

10. Ibid, 12.

11. Sideeque M.A. Veliankode, *Doomsday Portents and Prophecies* (Scarborough, Canada: Al-Attique, 1999), 2771

12. Ayatullah Baqir al-Sadr and Ayatullah Murtada Mutahhari, *The Awaited Savior*, (Karachi, Islamic Seminary Publications), prologue, 4, 5.

13. Muhammad ibn Izzat, *Muhammad 'Arif, Al Mahdi and the End of Time* (London: Dar Al-Taqwa, 1997), 4.

14. Abdulrahman Kelani, *The Last Apocalypse, An Islamic Perspective*, (Fustat, 2003), 34-35.

15. Ibn Hajar al-Haythami, *Al-Qawl al-Mukhtasar fi'Alamat al-Mahdi al-Muntazar*, 50, as quoted by Harun Yahya, *The End Times and the Mahdi* (Clarkesville Katoons, 2003), 96.

16. For an excellent history study of these Mahdist movements, see Dr. Timothy Furnish's work, *Holiest Wars* (Santa Barbara: Praeger, 2005).

CHAPTER 10: OUR RESPONSE

1. Dr. David R. Reagan, "The Wars of the End Times," Lamb and Lion Ministries, http://christinprophecy.org/articles/the-wars-of-the-end-times/.

2. 2017 World Watch List: https://www.opendoorsusa.org/christian-persecution/world-watch-list/.

CHAPTER 11: THE GRAND CLIMAX

1. See for example, Dave Garrison, *A Wind in the House of Islam* (Monument, CO: Wigtake Resources, 2014).

2. Dr. R. L. Hymers, Jr., "Tribulation and Revival," a sermon preached at the Baptist Tabernacle of Los Angeles, August 23, 2009, http://www.rlhymersjr.com/Online_Sermons/2009/082309PM_TribulationRevival.html.

3. Adam Clarke, Commentary on the Bible (1831), https://www.studylight.org/commentaries/acc/psalms-2.html.

CHAPTER 12: RISING TO THE TIMES

1. Tariq Tahir, "North Korean defector describes undergoing a forced abortion and the harrowing scenes as she watched prison dogs eat dead prisoners who had starved to death at her labour camp," *Daily Mail*, December 12, 2017, http://www.dailymail.co.uk/news/article-5170451/North-Korean-defector-says-forced-abortion.html.

2. Stoyan Zaimov, N. Korean Defector Recalls Screams of Pregnant Mothers During Forced Abortions; Inmates Used as Dog Food," *Christian Post*, December 13, 2017, https://www.christianpost.com/news/n-korean-defector-recalls-screams-of-pregnant-mothers-during-forced-abortions-inmates-used-as-dog-food-209998/.

3. https://www.thebalance.com/pareto-s-principle-the-80-20-rule-2275148; https://betterexplained.com/articles/understanding-the-pareto-principle-the-8020-rule/.

4. Kissinger, Henry, Colin S Gray, and G. R. Sloan, *Geopolitics, Geography, and Strategy* (Portland: Frank Cass Publishers, 1999), http://web.newworldencyclopedia.org/entry/Geopolitics.

5. Ian Johnston, "Climate change increases the risk of war, scientists prove," *Independent*, July 25, 2016, http://www.independent.co.uk/environment/climate-change-war-risk-increase-syria-isis-heatwave-drought-a7155401.html.

CHAPTER 13: A MISSIONARY FOR THE TIMES

1. Matthew Soerens and Daniel Darling, "The Gospel and Immigration," *Gospel Coalition*, May 1, 2012, https://www.thegospelcoalition.org/article/the-gospel-and-immigration/.

Giving Back

If you would like to contribute a one-time gift or give monthly to Antecessor, the ministry Nathan directs, please go to antecessor.org/give.

If you would like to become a monthly financial supporter of Nathan and Lorraine Graves please go to christar.org/give/projects/where-needed-most/support-a-worker/. Once there, enter ID # 322.

All gifts are tax deductible.

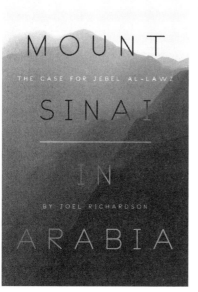

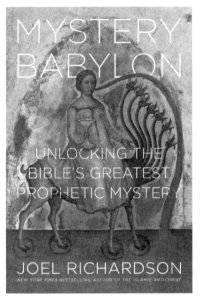

Antecessor is committed to helping churches and mission organizations successfully reach affected people in disasters. It is a bridge by providing the necessary services that will help enable emergency responders do their work more effectively. In short, Antecessor works to help improve disaster preparedness and response by

- Strengthening responders' capacity to mobilize proactively before, during and after a crises

- Maintaining a virtual network of contacts and resources it is able to mobilize in a crisis

- Acting as a communications bridge between people in need and others who want to support them during crises

Antecessor walks with those on the front lines of a crisis. It works to provide those helping with services before crises arise, during crises and post crisis transition, into the reconstruction phase. Its services, training, linkages and pre-coordination will facilitate your goals of moving from the disaster into long-term impact.

For more information or to give a tax-deductible gift,
go to https://antecessor.org/site/.